Playing

the Hand
that's Dealt
to You

A Guide
For
Parents
Of
Children
with
Special
Needs

Playing The Hand
That's Dealt To You

**A Guide For Parents
Of Children
With Special Needs**

*To all you folks
in St. Joe's PICU,
God bless you for
all you do for us!
Janet L Morel*

*by***Janet Morel**

illustrations by **Francois Poisson & Janet Morel**

Canmore Press

Canmore Press, P.O. Box 510794, Melbourne Beach, FL 32951-0794

Published 2000

Printed in the United States of America on archival paper with vegetable ink.

© All artwork is copyrighted and owned by Janet Morel.
Illustrations by Francois Poisson; mechanical drawings by Janet Morel.

© Cover photo by Carrie Lammers.

© Cover graphics and design by Lyn Cope-Robinson.

© Layout and design by Canmore Press.

©1987 *Welcome to Holland* by Emily Perl Kingsley; all rights reserved. Used with permission.

©*The Dream Keeper* by Langston Hughes from COLLECTED POEMS by Langston Hughes Copyright owned by the Estate of Langston Hughes. Reprinted by permission of Alfred A Knopf, a Division of Random House, Inc.

Toy designs on pages 43, 49, and 54 were graciously given by Cheryl Sjostrom.

Toy Adapter, page 53, invented by Jamie Dote-Kwan who has given all special parents the right to copy and use.

Library of Congress Cataloging-in-Publication Data

Morel, Janet, 1961-
    Playing the hand that's dealt to you : a guide for parents of children with special needs / by Janet Morel.
        p.cm.
    Includes bibliographical references and index.
    ISBN 1-887774-07-6 (alk. paper)
    1. Parents of handicapped children--Attitudes. 2. Parents of handicapped children--Psychology. 3. Handicapped children--Care. 4. Handicapped children--Family relationships. 5. Handicapped children--Education. I. Title.
    HQ759.913 . M67 2000
    649'.151--dc21
                                                                00-031190
                                                                CIP
ISBN (Quality paper) 1-887774-07-6

Table of Contents

Acknowledgements

I wish to thank the many special parents who contributed ideas, instructions, and poems often written to me on scraps of paper. I have done due diligence in trying to locate the original authors of these works through word of mouth, library research, copyright records, and on-line searches but with partial success. However, they contribute so strongly to the book that I chose to include them even though the originators could not be located. Considering the spirit of the book, it is my hope this will be acceptable. Any and all net profit from the sales of the book will be used for subsequent printing or donated to charitable causes as the law allows.

I would especially like to thank Eileen Payne, Jamie Dote-Kwan, Cheryl Sjostrom and Gina Gregory as the professionals who provided me with crucial information. It is Jamie Dote-Kwan who so willingly provided the directions for and permission to use her Toy Adapter on page 53. Cheryl Sjostrom's clever and invaluable toy designs include the Portable Toy Hanger, Plate Switch, and the Lighted Happy Face.

Also deserving of my deepest thanks are: my mother, for watching the kids while I typed; my husband, for understanding when the laundry wasn't done; Rebecca, for not getting too upset when I said I'd play with her in one minute and I took ten; Dana, for bringing me to a deeper understanding of love and life; and Dr. Rima McLeod for getting this all started. Lastly, many thanks to my publisher, Lyn Cope-Robinson, for getting this all finished!

Note To The Reader
Permission/Disclaimer

The contents of this book were compiled from many sources, both professional and amateur. The author wishes the reader, should she or he be the parent, caretaker, or professional provider of a special needs child, to find encouragement in this book. The reader assumes all responsibility to consult with a professional regarding the use of any information contained herein. The author gives permission for the reader to copy and modify her lists for a personal *Information Book* as described in Chapter Six, pages 70-77.

Furthermore, the author assumes no responsibility or liability for the outcome or effect, positive or negative, of any infant stimulation or early childhood intervention activities or programs of any kind. The author also assumes no liability for harm, personal injury, or death caused by the use of any of the ideas contained in this book or of any homemade or purchased devices used by the affected party.

The author has received no compensation, monetary or otherwise, by any company or organization mentioned herein.

Preface

During my studies of Child Development and Counseling, it struck me that there were so many different theories of development. Each was built on a totally different premise and was very viable in its own right. However, whether it was Rogers, Piaget, Erikson, or Freud, all of the theories in their purest form seemed to lack in an important area on which another theory was based. I learned to gather from each theory that material which applied to the situation or problem at hand. This means that all theories can be useful tools on which to lean. I mention this because that is the way I wish for this book to be used. Parenting a child with disabilities can be such a different experience for each person. The children are all individuals, the parents are unique to themselves, the disabilities are so diverse, and the resources available can vary greatly. It would be impossible to write a practical informational guide that would encompass every need. This book is simply a compilation of information that I found useful in my own circumstances. Much of it can be useful for the development of all children, regardless of their abilities. I write it so the readers might be able to take what may be useful to them and apply it to their own needs. I also hope that some of the ideas presented may spark new ideas that may result in happier, more productive lives for the children and their parents.

You will find that I have used a more familiar way of referring to children by using the words "him" and "her," instead of "the child." I recognize that your own special little charge is not just an object to be manipulated, but a beautiful little person with a spirit and personality all his own. For ease of reading I choose one gender at a time.

I

Facing the Challenges
of Your Child's Disability

Great necessities call out great virtues.
— Abigail Adams

As I was growing up, my family spent many evenings at the dining room table playing games. Monopoly and Scrabble made their occasional appearances, but nothing was as popular as card games. My father liked poker best. We children enjoyed bringing out the red, white, and blue colored chips to use as our play money. By the time I was five years old I knew that a full house beats a straight. My father also taught me another very important lesson. You can't ask for another set of cards to be dealt to you. You must accept the cards you receive from the dealer and do the best you possibly can with what you have in your hand. I've used that advice in many areas of my life, especially when life dealt me an unexpected blow.

Our daughter, Dana, was born six weeks prematurely with congenital toxoplasmosis. It is a disease caused by a microorganism that is passed to humans by cat litter and undercooked meats or unwashed produce. If the organism enters an expectant mother's body and the mother has never contracted toxoplasma before, the parasite can make its way to the fetus. The fetus has no immune system with which to fight off the organism, and it can do a lot of harm if not treated quickly. The doctors were able to determine that I had contracted the disease during the first trimester of my pregnancy. The microorganism had therefore had many months to do a lot of damage to the tissue of Dana's brain and to the retinas of her eyes. To complicate things more, she also suffered from lack of oxygen during a difficult birth. That caused even greater damage to her brain. At the time of this writing, she is eight years old. She does not walk, sit, roll over, talk, toilet or feed herself. She sees only shadows and motion. We have had more than our share of hospitalizations and heartaches, doubts and disappointments. Yet, we have found that it is still possible to maintain happy, positive lives for ourselves as a family with a child with disabilities.

The past eight years have brought many new experiences and insights. Becoming a special parent means instantly becoming a part of a very unique subculture in one's community, an experience one may or may not appreciate. Suddenly, there are new people involving themselves in our lives. Social workers, doctors and nurses, service care providers and therapists seem to make up a constant parade that runs through our days. Doctors have few answers to our many questions. Professionals tell us how to raise our child. There are new terms to learn — practically a whole new language spoken. We are expected to attend thousands of meetings and appointments. Other people we have never met are automatically expected to be our friends because they also have a child with a disability. In other words, we face not only sorrow and sense of loss due to our child's disability, but also frustration brought about by the situation. Unfortunately, there is not a lot of help out there. There are few organized sources of information for some of the basics of how to live a rich life with a precious special child. The parent is required to do the digging and research for herself or himself, or just to learn by life's experiences.

Usually, the best sources of information are other parents who have put in their time or done the digging already. There is so much that an exceptional parent needs to know, and so much that can be learned from others. This is why I wrote this book. I have learned more pertinent information from other parents than from any of the professionals involved in my life. Many of the ideas and insights have been harvested from the bountiful knowledge of those who have had to learn for themselves. I will also share what the experiences of my own life with my daughter have taught me.

Need I even say that much is expected of any new parent when it comes to the care of a new baby? However, you as a special parent have even more responsibility placed on you for the development of your child. You are now expected to stimulate your little one in such a way so as to help him maximize his potential development. Don't fret. You'll find a lot of ideas in these pages. This stimulation is so very important and beneficial to him, and it can be a fun part of your new life. Furthermore, the play that happens between you and your child is a crucial part of creating a bond that builds a strong family — a bond that is sometimes difficult to attain with a child who is developmentally delayed.

There are other issues in parenting besides just bonding and stimulation, though. Parents of special children deal with many

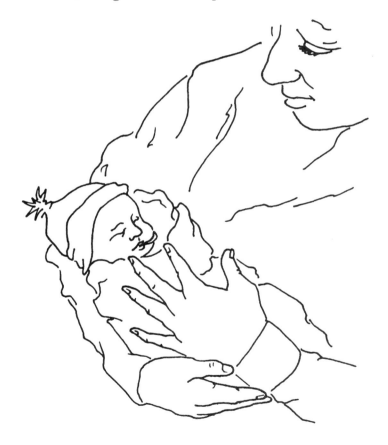

fears about the future. We fear what may happen when we can no longer give our children the kind of care they require. I, for instance, am a petite woman, and lifting my daughter is already causing me physical ailments. It will not be much longer before I will not be able to lift her. I ask myself, "What I will do then?" There may come a time for out-of-home placement or in-home care. Then, there is the ultimate concern of the future. What will happen when I am no longer living? Who will take care of her? How can she survive without my love and attention? The good news is there are many options for a parent needing help in providing care. **You can get the help you need.** You can also gain some peace of mind by planning ahead and getting everything in order for the future should something happen to you. Planning your estate now can give you a great sense of relief and comfort.

If you haven't already discovered it, there is a new word in the "new language" you must now learn that will come up again and again. That word is "advocacy." This means being a good representative for your child and knowing how to get what he needs. It also means getting that to which you and he are entitled. If you never had to act as anyone's advocate before, brace yourself, because you will now. You will have to become the mother bear protecting her young. You will need to learn how to get quality medical care. You will need to know how to maintain good medical records. You will need to make decisions about an appropriate education for your child and then exhaust a lot of energy to make sure he gets the education you know he needs. This is yet another major stress factor for parents, but it does not always have to be a nasty battle. Most professionals will gladly strive for the same goals as the parents, if the parents can stay rational and calm, and present their desires in a professional manner. You'll find a few rules of thumb here to help you get started.

Above all else, I want to encourage you on your journey through this challenging life. Maintaining a positive outlook is essential to maintaining your sanity. That is just as important as any of the tips or ideas you may find useful. In fact, I would go so far as to say it is the most important part of living a happy and successful life, especially while playing the special hand that life has dealt to you.

Welcome to Holland
— Emily Perl Kingsley

I am often asked to describe the experience of raising a child with a disability — to try to help people who have not shared that unique experience to understand it, to imagine how it would feel, it's like this. . .

When you're going to have a baby, it's like planning a fabulous vacation trip — to Italy. You buy a bunch of guide books and make your wonderful plans. The Coliseum. The Michelangelo David. The gondolas in Venice. You may learn some handy phrases in Italian. It's all very exciting.

After months of eager anticipation, the day finally arrives. You pack your bags and off you go. Several hours later, the plane lands. The stewardess comes in and says, "Welcome to Holland."

"Holland?!?" you say. "What do you mean, Holland?? I signed

up for Italy! I'm supposed to be in Italy. All my life I've dreamed of going to Italy."

But there's been a change in the flight plan. They've landed in Holland and there you must stay.

The important thing is that they haven't taken you to a horrible, disgusting, filthy place, full of pestilence, famine, and disease. It's just a different place.

So, you must go out and buy new guide books. And you must learn a whole new language. And you will meet a whole new group of people you would never have met.

It's just a <u>different</u> place. It's slower-paced than Italy, less flashy than Italy. But after you've been there for a while and you catch your breath, you look around... and you begin to notice that Holland has windmills... Holland has tulips. Holland even has Rembrandts.

But everyone you know is busy coming and going from Italy... and they're all bragging about what a wonderful time they had there. And for the rest of your life, you will say, "Yes, that's where I was supposed to go. That's what I had planned."

And the pain of that will never, ever, ever go away... because the loss of that dream is a very very significant loss.

But... if you spend your life mourning the fact that you didn't get to Italy, you may never be free to enjoy the very special, the very lovely things... about Holland.

2

CREATING A SYSTEM OF SUPPORT THAT WILL HELP YOU SURVIVE

Give us grace and strength to forbear and to persevere. Give us courage and gaiety and the quiet mind, spare to us our friends.
— Robert Louis Stevenson

Why are some families that face special challenges so content when there are so many other exceptional families struggling with anger, divorce, stress, isolation, emotional distress, etc.? We've all had negative feelings and experiences. Why have some been able to come out on top? I'm sure the answer is not simple, but there are a few things I can point out.

When Dana was very young, we vowed that we were not going to let her disabilities stop us. We were going to take those vacations. We would go on picnics in the park. We would even learn to fly an airplane. I strongly believe that the best thing I can do for my daughter, Dana, is to give her a mother who is content. Let me state that again. The very best thing that you can do for your son or daughter is to make sure that you are content. Stephen

Covey in his book, *The Seven Habits of Highly Effective People*, calls this "Sharpening the Saw." He tells the story of a man trying very hard to saw down a tree. It becomes very hard work. The more he saws, the more difficult the work becomes. If he would just take a moment to sharpen his saw, the work would be a lot easier and the tree would be down a lot sooner. So we, too, have to take the time in our own lives to feed our emotional, physical, social, and spiritual needs. Only then will we be prepared and strong and happy to handle those things that are required of us. Only when we are full can we give to those around us. It's a nice thought, but how do you take time out to enjoy life when there are so many demands placed on you? The answer is that it takes a conscious effort.

I am reminded of one particularly trying period in our lives. Dana has a VP shunt. This is a valve that has been surgically placed in her brain to drain excess fluid. Occasionally, these shunts malfunction and the results can be fatal. One day it was obvious that a problem was developing. She was suddenly lethargic and vomiting. Both are signs of a shunt malfunction. I ended up with her in an emergency clinic with a surgeon I didn't know, making plans for emergency surgery that afternoon in order to repair the shunt.

Now, let me put this into the context of our lives at that moment in time. My husband, Rob, had just finished an eighteen-month assignment in another state. During all of that time he managed to fly home for the weekends. I was working a full-time job and taking care of two little ones by myself. Rob had racked up enough frequent-flier miles that we had been able to plan a vacation to Hawaii for all four of us. The plane tickets, of course, had to be purchased many months in advance in order to take advantage of the free airfare. We were so excited! This was the first vacation ever for just the four of us. There would be no other family members along with whom to synchronize schedules. It would be just us, and we really needed the time together away from the demands of life. The months of waiting made the anticipation increase with every day, until it was almost unbearable. Sunny beaches, here we come! Snorkeling, sun bathing, swimming, lounging, and all of the other typical things tourists do in Hawaii were just waiting for us! Cawabunga! We were to leave in two days.

The waiting room in the hospital emergency ward was mocking me. As I feared for my daughter's life, everything around me seemed to dash my dreams to the ground. There was a man sitting next to me wearing a Hawaiian shirt. The T. V. was on. There was a football game being played. It was being broadcast from Hawaii. When it was over, a young mother changed the channel for her child. There were the Muppets staring me in the face, singing a lively tropical tune. They were all telling me that I was not going to be able to go to Hawaii on my dream vacation. Worse, I might lose my daughter.

Dana made it through just fine. Miraculously, she was home after one night's stay in the hospital. We even had the doctor's consent and recommendation that we stick with our plans and go on the trip. She could recover just as well on the beaches as at home (probably better!). If there was a problem, there are hospitals in Hawaii, too.

Off we went, with our child who had half of her hair shaved off and bloody bandages on her head and abdomen. She was not a pretty sight. We rethought our plans. Dana would have to stay on dry ground at all times. She couldn't even float in her blow-up boat and ride along with us while we snorkeled. We would have to take turns. One of us would stay with her while the other went swimming. We would have to keep her somewhat quiet, so we wouldn't do much sight-seeing. We had to make sure no sand got into the wounds and that the bandages were clean. Worse yet, we would have to put up with the stares and contempt of others.

In the end, was it really worth all of the trouble? Was it worth going when we had to change our plans? Did we actually enjoy ourselves? Did we come home renewed? You bet! The truth is, I was so relaxed when I came back that I must have worked at half speed for two weeks. Refreshed. Renewed. At peace. Hang loose, baby!

All that, just to say that we must manage to find a way through the inconveniences of having a child with special needs so that we, as parents, can be fulfilled. Notice that I say "through", not "around". It is sometimes not possible to get completely away from the demands of our life. For example, it can be very inconvenient to bring along a wheel chair and a child who can't feed or toilet herself. However, the rewards of working through the inconveniences are more than worth the trials. It may just take us longer to do something than other families. We may have to do things differently. We may have to put up with many inconveniences, but we do it. We do it. We do it because we have to. This, almost above all else, is a key element in making our lives bearable, or even enjoyable!

Another key is to establish a good system of support around you. You will need others to be there for you if times get tough. You must realize that most of the people you will depend on have never been in your shoes and have a difficult time relating to your life or to the demands placed upon you. They may even be a little afraid of what they don't know. Until they have an opportunity to become better acquainted, they may have a hard time being around your family. If you want to break down barriers and help them to feel more comfortable with you and your family, it is extremely important to try to maintain as much normalcy in your lives as possible. Support systems are an essential component of your life as a parent of a child with special needs. One of the greatest complaints of exceptional parents is having feelings of isolation. Sometimes it is the severity of the child's disability that causes a feeling of uneasiness in others. Sometimes it is the parent who drives people away. I have a friend who has almost completely estranged herself from all others because all she ever talks about are the struggles she has with her son who is disabled. She often speaks about him with disrespect and sarcasm. This makes others very uncomfortable to be around her. They have a hard enough time relating to her experiences in the first place. When she dwells on the negative and speaks of nothing else but her "abnormal" son, barriers go up between her and others. It even makes me uncomfortable, when I, of all people, should be understanding. The more parents can treat their lives and their child with normalcy, the more comfortable others will feel about being around them and helping them.

Our family is fortunate to have a very good support system. Our extended families live hundreds of miles away, but they have accepted Dana. However, I admit that is not the case for every family. Many family members have difficulty accepting a special child into the family. I met a man who had never been to see his two-year-old grandson because he considered him a freak and was afraid he would not know how to act. It made my heart ache, not only for this man who had lost an opportunity to enrich his life with joy, but also for the parents of the boy. They must have felt so rejected and alone. Whatever the reason, be it distance or discomfort, grandparents or other family members may not always be available to help you in time of need. You may need to create a second family of support.

We happen to share a strong faith in God, and I would be remiss if I didn't mention that as a major source of peace and strength in our lives. It would be impossible to express how much our faith and church shape our attitudes about the difficulties we face and how they enable us to press on. Yet, it is also important to understand that by being involved in the church we have been given a circle of friends that share similar values. We are able to share ourselves more than just superficially with others. We have also discovered that many people who seemed cold or timid toward Dana were actually yearning for a chance to learn how to reach out to her. When we have asked for baby-sitting, many have thanked us for the opportunity to care for her for a few hours and allow us the privilege of having a date. We try to repay them by caring for their children once in a while (a very simple exchange, and what a great way to encourage other children to be accepting of differences!). These same people who share in our faith and Bible studies, as well as in our baby-sitting exchange, are now the ones who are there for us when we face the difficult trials of surgeries or denied services. At first it requires some effort to help people appreciate our life and our needs. I have often had to share my life and feelings quite openly to my friends and to entire church congregations so that they can understand where I am coming from. Taking that time to build special friendships and trust my feelings to others has created the bonds with others that have been a vital source of support.

I am sure there are many parts of the country that do not have a great awareness of the needs of the disabled community. If you need help creating an awareness in your community, church, or other group, you can contact any of the organizations in your area that provide services to children with special needs and their families. The people there can help you establish a system of support that can provide the help that would otherwise be missing. They should have resources available for you to encourage disability awareness in those people around you.

Parent-to-parent organizations and support groups are another great source of information, friendship, acceptance, and understanding. It is in these groups and relationships that you will find the type of understanding that only someone in similar circumstances can provide. They have comforted me when I have felt like a terrible mother for being angry with Dana when she does not sleep well. It is such a relief to hear other mothers say, "Me, too!" Some support groups, however, seem to turn into gripe sessions, and negative feelings (especially about doctors) are flung about irrationally with no regard for empathy toward others. Those are the groups I avoid because I leave them feeling worse than when I came. In such circumstances, you might do better to join a mother/child play-group than a support group for exceptional parents. You may find these groups offer more positive and normal interaction with other parents, at the same time building a support system. Still, many special parental support groups emphasize positive sharing and exchange of good quality information. Many bring in motivational speakers or medical personnel to answer questions. If you cannot find such a group in your area, start one. It is most likely there are many other parents in search of quality interaction and compassion.

Connecting with other parents need not be as structured an effort in some peoples lives. You will probably also find yourself just coming across other parents of children with special needs in your normal day-to-day activities. This is one of my favorite ways to meet others that can relate to me. In fact, it has been through casual acquaintance that I have met those parents who have become my mentors. Because their children are a little older than mine, they have already covered the ground that may be new to me. They reassure me that I'll overcome any obstacles sent my way, and they connect me with people who can really get some answers for me. These friends have been invaluable supports.

A new source of support and information that has been gaining increased popularity is the World Wide Web. One particularly remarkable website is http://www. familyvillage. wisc. edu. The site can link you up to more resources than you ever thought possible. It can guide you to make connections with other parents. You can look up information about a specific diagnosis. There is an extensive book and resource list, and even a list of on-line sites from which you can purchase special toys or equipment. Other topics covered on this website are hospitals, worship, schools, and recreation and leisure. In short, it is an excellent place to start in your quest for information, services, and other help. Another good source on the web is the *Exceptional Parent Magazine* site, or http://www. eparent. com. Although it is mostly a promotion of the magazine itself, it does provide some connections with other resources, as well as advice. The most remarkable part of the site is the extensive library listing where you may be able to find "just the right book" for what you need to know.

Obviously, there are many different ways to go about creating a system of support. All of these are merely building blocks. Any or all of them may work for you, depending on your personality. The important thing is that the support is established. Be aware that it will take effort, and it will mean getting involved. Before all else, you will need to take care of yourself. Also, be aware that you may need to share your story with others to break down barriers. You will certainly need to invite others into your life. In short, it's up to you to be enough of a friend to others in order to make sure someone knows enough and cares enough about you to be there when times get tough.

— Author Unknown

If you have learned to walk
A little more sure-footedly than I,
Be patient with my stumbling then
And know that only as I do my best and try
May I attain the goal
For which we both are striving.
If through experience, your soul
Has gained heights which I
As yet in dim-lit vision see,
Hold out your hand and point the way,
Lest from its straightness I should stray,
And walk a mile with me.

3

HELPING YOUR CHILD
REACH HIS GREATEST POTENTIAL

The great thing in this world is not so much where we stand,
as in what direction we are moving.
— Goethe

Stimulating the senses and the mind during the early years is essential for any child, but especially for a child with special needs. It is so easy, especially if you have a quiet child, to allow the child to sit in a room by himself or herself while you stand at the kitchen sink washing the dishes. Although reality demands that household chores be done, don't give in to the temptation to always take this "easier" path. The child development expert Piaget strongly stated that a child that is given many opportunities for stimulation and exploration will be more likely to reach a higher level of functioning and intelligence. In addition, stimulating your child can be a wonderful way for you to build a close bond with him as you play and explore the world together.

Nothing can fully replace a formal and professional early intervention infant stimulation program, which may be available through your county or state. A lot of attention has been given to the success of these programs. The actor/director Rob Reiner believes so strongly in this type of intervention and education that he created his own foundation called *I Am Your Child* for supporting programs that seek to improve the potential for children through early childhood stimulation. In addition to seeking this type of service for your child, you may wish to try some of the ideas in this chapter at home. You may want to incorporate them into a formal home program given by a teacher or therapist, or you may want to just have a little fun with your child. Here are a few ideas for stimulating sight, touch, smell, sound, taste, small movement, and large movement. Although most of these ideas are very simple, it is my recommendation that you have your child's regular doctor or therapist give his or her approval before you use them.

SIGHT

There is a reason why mobiles have traditionally become a part of every infant's bedroom. They provide something interesting to look at. Child development experts agree that in the very early stages of development, sight is the way a child receives the most input. Sight is the basic building block for all learning.

If you don't already have a mobile, get one, even if your child may be visually impaired. Black and white patterns are best, or brightly colored objects. With close supervision, you can even gently tie a string from your baby's foot or wrist to the mobile so that any time she kicks she will see motion. This is also an excellent way to teach cause and effect. The patterns and colors of the mobile are so interesting to a child, and they can be translated to other parts of the child's surroundings. **Brightly colored furniture and walls provide a lot of opportunity for visual stimulation.** Christmas lights strung on the walls add an even more brilliant touch. *Be careful, however, to string them out of baby's reach and not on the bed or crib for risk of strangulation.*

How many hours do you spend in the car going to and from appointments or errands? All the while the child is staring at the seat in front of him. Why not make some cards with black and white patterns that can be pinned to the seat back in front of him? **Patterns can be stripes, concentric circles, wavy lines, or dots.** Be creative. Babies are also attracted to simple face patterns.

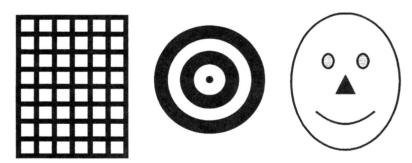

Small plastic bottles or finger puppets placed over the lighted end of pen lights make great lighted wands for the child's eyes to track. Move these slowly in front of the child's face about 9-12 inches away. Encourage him to follow the moving light with his eyes. Ask him to reach out and grasp the object, or help him to do so.

Hang plastic Christmas tree "icicles" from a made-at-home PVC-pipe Portable Toy Hanger (see Chapter Four for construction instructions). *Do this under supervision so the child will not ingest the icicles.*

Fish can be very attractive to children. **A bowl of goldfish can provide hours of stimulation.** There are also many different kinds of aquarium fish that have fluorescent colors that glow especially brightly when placed under a light. Their slow movements are easily tracked.

It is surprising how many things can be found in the home that can be stimulating: flashlights reflected off of pie tins, stained glass "light catchers," mirrors, toys that light up, crystal prisms in a window, shadows on the wall, even the clothing we wear. The trick is to be aware of our surroundings and bring a variety of experiences to our children.

TOUCH

Touch is essential for children to thrive. The famous researcher, H. F. Harlow, used monkeys to document the outcome of development when the mother is not present. Those infant monkeys who were raised in an environment that did not provide the stimulus of touch were profoundly affected in their mental, physical, and emotional development. Many could not survive. However, those monkeys who had a type of "surrogate" mother, even though it was just an inanimate object like a stuffed animal, had a much more positive outcome in their development. There was even documentation many centuries ago of the differences in children who were raised in institutional environments without the benefit of a mother's care. It is fascinating that such a natural thing as just cuddling, rocking, and caressing our baby can make a great difference in the baby's ability to thrive.

We, as parents, need to be sure to provide stimulation in order to insure the best outcome in our own children's development. As mentioned above, chores must be done, and children must learn to be patient and entertain themselves. However, it is important to continually seek opportunities to help our children receive the tactile stimulation they need. Following are a few simple ideas you can use.

Rub different textures over the palms and fingers of the child's hands. These can be found anywhere: baby brushes, plush toys, squeaky pet toys with bumpy surfaces (such as a rubber porcupine), pumice stone, a smooth juice glass, feathers, sand paper, and masking tape. This would be called a "passive" activity in which the child does not exert much effort. A similar "active" activity, in which he takes an active part, is to place a tray in front of him and have him reach out and touch different objects you place in the tray. He may have a tray on his high chair, walker, or wheelchair. It is preferable to have a tray with about a 1-2 inch depth. One can even use a cake pan, or a shallow plastic tub. Just let him explore. You may need to give a little help guiding his hand. Please note that children with visual impairments are normally tactually sensitive and may have difficulty tolerating this activity at first, but it is well worth the effort to be patient with him. Give him a chance to get used to the tactile stimulation and to continue to try. Some items that can be placed in the tray include rice, dried black beans or peas (I recommend these for their small size. Larger pinto beans may likely end up lodged in a child's nostril if not carefully monitored), oatmeal (what a wonderful mess!), pudding (even messier!), shaving cream, packaging pellets (again, watch that they do not go in the mouth), Cheerios, cotton balls, wooden blocks, straw, raffia, or Easter grass. One of Dana's favorite activities during the warm summer months is simply splashing in a tray of water. This, of course, should also be closely supervised, especially if the child does not yet have enough head control to keep his or her face out of the water. This activity need not be confined to manual (hand) stimulation. Try setting it up so that your child can splash with her feet, or even her entire body! I remember from my childhood how wonderful it was to sit in a bin of whole grain while visiting a farm. Even fast food restaurants

have cashed in on our love of stimulating touch because they provide play areas full of little colorful balls for the kids to "swim" through!

A trip to the grocery store can be a wonderful source of inspiration for a variety of stimulating experiences. Just think about the fresh produce department. Let your child feel the textures of the citrus fruit, the broccoli, or the pineapple. Don't forget to pinch a few and smell. Other departments can be equally interesting. Together you can feel how round, smooth, and hard the eggs are. Potato chip bags provide another unusual texture, and they have a great crackly, crunchy sound. How cold is the ice cream? How rough is the log for the fire? The possibilities are endless.

Another easy way of providing a variety of tactile experiences is what I call a "feel-y" quilt. Instructions for this quilt are found in Chapter Four. It simply consists of squares of differently textured fabric sewn together into a big blanket.

Lastly, let me recommend learning a few simple massage techniques that can be used to relax your child after a bath or before bed. What a wonderful way to spend quality time bonding with your child. I do not pretend to be a massage expert, but the following are a few examples I learned and highly recommend from the book *Infant Massage* by Vilmala Schneider McClure. Starting with the legs, because these are usually the least intrusive and sensitive to a child, gently lay your hands (palms down) on your child's ankles. Slowly glide them upward to the hips and down again, being careful to maintain contact at all times. Repeat this motion slowly and rhythmically several times. Then, without losing contact between your hands and your little one, slowly move your hands to his chest. Glide your right hand to the his right shoulder, crossing over the chest and then back down to the left hip. Likewise, glide your left hand across to his left shoulder and back. Repeat these motions in an "X" pattern rhythmically and reciprocally, again making sure not to lose contact between your two hands and your child. You can then move your hands to his shoulders and glide your hands down to his wrists and back again, much like you did for the legs. These are just a few simple examples. If you wish to learn more, McClure's book is an excellent resource.

SMELL AND TASTE

Just close your eyes for a moment and try to remember what the world smells like after rain. There is such a rich world of scents that we take for granted because we rely so heavily on sight. Encourage your child to discover and enjoy them for himself. You will be amazed what the two of you may discover together.

- Let her help wash the dog or do the laundry.

- Give him a garden of his own.

- Offer a variety of foods.

- Take walks through a wheat field, an oak grove, a pine forest, or on a beach.

- Take a stroll through a flower garden and discover how many different scents there are.

- Stick your thumbnail into the orange or lemon rind and let her smell.

- Talk about the different smells coming from the kitchen: warm baked bread, spaghetti sauce, cookies, pot roast, etc. You can use this to build anticipation to try new tastes.

- Try out various perfumes and have your child smell them, or let him smell his shampoo, conditioner, and soap while in the bath. You may also want to try some aroma therapy oils or candles in your home and discover which your child responds to most favorably.

● Scratch-N-Sniff stickers or books make great ideas for birthday gifts when friends don't know what to give.

As you may already know, smell and taste are related senses. Take advantage of this and make the most of mealtimes, pointing out to your child all of the different sensational experiences involved. How does it smell? Is it bumpy or smooth? Chewy or soft? Sweet or sour? Hot or cold? What color is it? Does it make a funny noise when it lands on the floor or is pitched into Mommy's hair? As a final note, keep in mind that it is very important to provide a variety of food tastes and textures not only for sensory stimulation, but also to foster oral and communicative skills as discussed in another section.

SOUND

Studies show that a baby recognizes her mother's voice even while still in the womb. If a baby can tune in so specifically to a sound while in such a protected environment, just imagine what the world must seem like to her after she is born! Babies are usually very aware of the slightest differences in sound around them. Think of how your child responds when you use a sing-song voice to her. How does she act when you speak loudly? Fast? Softly? She usually will change her own body movement in rhythm and response to your different voices. This is the beginning of language development. For that reason, sound stimulation is very important for helping your child develop the skills of communication that will be so essential to enriching her life in the future. Here are just a few ideas to get you started.

- Collect used 35 mm. film canisters. Fill them with different objects such as rice, jingle bells, or paper clips. You can hang them from a toy hanger so that your little one can kick them or bat at them to hear the different sounds. Then, your child can hold them and shake them. You can ask your toddler to guess what's inside.

- Securely sew large jingle bells to a seven-inch strip of nylon webbing and sew Velcro fasteners to the ends so that the bells may be strapped onto the child's wrist or ankles. This is good for motor development, too, because the child soon learns that when he moves it makes a marvelous sound, and he will be motivated to move more.

  Caution: Do not allow your child to chew on this toy because he could choke if a bell were to come loose.

- Teacher's bells with handles are sturdy enough to bang around and they also encourage grasping.

- Provide opportunities for your child to play with any battery-operated toys that squawk, bark, beep, bang, yip, or growl, especially if the toy is adapted with a plate switch (instructions in Chapter Four) so she can have control over the noisy toy.

- My First Sony is a child's cassette player built to be sturdy enough for even toddlers to play with. This can open up a whole world of auditory stimulation. There are cassettes with children's music and children's stories. There are even cassettes of different kinds of sounds, such as sawing wood and using a blender. Teacher's supply stores are good places to find these. You can also make up your own tapes of sounds your child is familiar with and enjoys. Relatives can record messages and send them for her to hear. You can record your child's own vocalizations and play them back to her. She'll love hearing her own voice and sounds, especially when laughter is played back!

When buying music cassettes for your child, don't limit yourself to browsing only through the children's selections. Classical music can be very complex and stimulating. Children especially seem to enjoy Mozart. In fact, Mozart's music has been proven to increase cognitive skills and is often played in classroom settings to increase the student's learning potential. I recommend vocal classical music because children are naturally attracted to the human voice.

- During your everyday activities, talk to your child about the sounds he is experiencing — cars on the highway, elevators, bells, the dishwasher running, or bath water filling the tub. You will have to remind yourself to constantly remain tuned in to your child's surroundings.

If your son or daughter is hearing impaired, do not automatically assume that sound stimulation will not be beneficial. Speak softly, but close to his ear. Gently shake a rattle or other similar toy near his ear, too. There may be some actual sensation of sound. Sound is made up of vibrations, and your child needs to experience those different vibrations and become familiar with them. In essence, he may experience sound differently, but he can still experience it.

FINE MOTOR

Fine motor skills are those skills that enable us to manipulate the hands and fingers, mouth and tongue. You use fine motor skills when you pick up a penny and when you write a letter. You use them when you sip a soda at the movie theater, eat some popcorn, and whisper to the person sitting next to you. **Fine motor skills are those skills that will eventually allow your child to have some control of his own life.** He will need to communicate his needs. He will also want to have some control over his environment. So, you can see how very important it is to stimulate and encourage these skills. He can begin by just being able to play with toys. The previous section on sensory stimulation has a lot of ideas that help tremendously in this area, but here are a few more.

What would motivate your child? Would it be learning to remove pegs from a pegboard? Would it be holding a plastic hammer and banging away on a metal pan lid? Both of these activities encourage grasping skills as does a teacher's bell with a small rounded handle.

Infant activity centers are great for manipulation skills. I'm sure you've seen these. Sometimes they are plastic boards. Sometimes they are soft play mats. They provide hours of fun entertainment and rich opportunities to squeeze, crank, roll, spin, and otherwise manipulate the colorful objects on them.

There are a variety of different types of switches available that your child could learn to use in order to turn on a battery-operated toy. Some are tactually sensitive plate switches of many sizes, colors, and shapes. Some have strings with beads tied to them to grasp and pull. There is one that is a curtain of metal beads that he can reach out to touch. Another that is a cylinder that he only has to gently rotate. These are all available from a company called Enabling Devices and Toys for Special Children™. You can find information about this company in the appendix.

How about putty, play dough, or puzzles? These can really strengthen those little fingers and encourage manipulation. Just have your child poke the dough. He can practice grasping by picking up different shapes molded out of the putty or dough. If puzzle pieces by themselves are too difficult, there are many available that have knobs, big or little, attached to the pieces.

Maybe your child would like to try to find little balls hidden in a bowl of rice. Try this yourself and see how interesting it feels! Once his dexterity increases, try smaller items, such as beads or beans. *Again, this will need supervision.* If your child is visually impaired, this type of activity is great for preparing him for Braille. Eventually, you can try this with such items as small safety pins or small beads.

My daughter likes to release and drop one-inch cube blocks onto a hard floor just to hear how they sound. It makes a mess, and I am constantly picking blocks up off of the floor and placing them back on her tray, but she is very motivated by this. Do whatever works!

Try having fun with a battery-operated pen that vibrates in little circles. This is another favorite in our household. Dana has difficulty holding on to the pen, so I help her draw by using my hands over hers. The vibrations are very stimulating and the pen encourages grasping.

Finger foods, such as hot dogs, bread sticks, and string cheese sticks, also motivate a child to grasp. You can build up the stick on a lollypop to make it easier to grasp by wrapping it in masking tape until the stick is about one-half inch in diameter. Tootsie Rolls work well, too. As long as we are on the subject of sweets, You can buy lollypop holders that are battery-operated so that they spin the pop or so that when your child bites down on the pop it will play music. After all of the eating is done, don't forget the battery-operated toothbrush. If you are tired of buying batteries (and you will be), infant toothbrush sets offer built-up handles and a variety of textures.

Piano keyboards and computers or typewriters encourage single-digit (finger) movement. The possibilities are endless.

Fine oral motor skills can be developed by offering a variety of textured foods, and by providing differently textured objects for the child's mouth and tongue to explore. Let's face it, pudding and ground chicken offer entirely different sensations! Remember the variety of textured objects you can use to rub along your baby's palms? Why not try some of them gently on her tongue or lips? Imagine how different a metal mirror must feel when compared to a toothbrush, a sponge, or even fur. Just make sure they are all clean!

Another fun exercise is to place peanut butter on your child's lips and let her try to lick it off. As her skill increases with this exercise, try putting some on the corners of her mouth. This is a great exercise for strengthening her tongue. It also helps her to become more skillful with her tongue to prepare for speech.

Dana had difficulty mastering drinking from a cup and still has a very strong sucking reflex. We decided to use that to her benefit and teach her to drink from a straw. Introducing the straw slowly to her by first inserting a narrow juice box straw into the hole of a juice nipple, we were able to offer a tactile sensation that was similar to the bottle, but she was challenged to accept larger quantities of juice at one time. Gradually, we were able to remove the nipple and then work up to a larger straw size. We did notice that she was able to get better lip closure around the straw if we offered it to her at the corner of her mouth at first. Now, she drinks from a straw as well as I do.

LARGE MOTOR

In addition to developing fine motor skills, children must use their larger muscles in order to maintain optimal health. These are the muscle groups that help us to swing our arms about, to kick, and to move around. Moving these muscles helps to keep the heart pumping and the blood flowing. Without his movement, the body will atrophy and become more susceptible to disease. This is especially a problem for our little ones who have cerebral palsy. Why is it that so many of these kids die too young? Experts suggest that a lot of it has to do with lack of movement. We must encourage the skills they need in order to get moving and live healthier lives.

Vestibular stimulation is often a package deal with large motor movement. It can be considered an added benefit. The term comes from the vestibules of the inner ear; the parts that help us sense movement through space. These are the parts of us that theme parks have capitalized on for generations. Why do you think we love roller coasters so much? Why do we like to spin around and go up and down. It is stimulating to our inner ear. For this reason, stimulating and encouraging large motor movement is probably the most enjoyable type of stimulation for all involved. It can be soothing, or interactive, or instructive, but always a lot of fun.

I don't know any child who does not enjoy a swing. If your child has physical limitations, you can swing with him on your lap. Adaptive swings can be purchased through Special Populations Catalog™, which is put out by Flaghouse™ (see Appendix). The swings are not cheap, but can open doors for your child. They are supportive enough that even little friends can help push the swing. Another alternative is a hammock. They are usually pretty inexpensive at your nearby import store. Mom and Dad, you'll love to have one, too!

When the weather is warm, or if you have access to an indoor pool, swimming is a marvelous activity. Again, all sorts of adaptive devices are available if your child needs help to float. There are swimsuits with floats built right in. There are also floats you can slip over the arms and legs of your child, and even floats that will just keep his head above water! The wonderful thing about the water is that it removes some gravitational pull and often frees a child to move more easily. You can even try physical therapy created especially for water play. Ask your child's therapist, if you have one, to develop this specialized home program with you. You might look up a local parent/child swimming class through parks and recreation departments. Some of the instructors have been trained to work with people with special needs.

Rhythmic dance with ribbons, hoops, or scarves encourages large movements. In fact, many of the fine arts are motivating and are being used more and more for the development of people with disabilities, as well as for their recreation. Painting, sculpting, drawing, dance, or playing an instrument (even as simple as a tambourine), are great incentives for movement, as well as expressive creativity. Music therapy has become a hot item recently. Do a little digging and see if there is a program in your area.

Large fitness balls have become very popular for young and old, and they are now readily available in toy stores, sports stores and mail order catalogs. They can cost anywhere from $25.00 to $120.00, depending on size and type. They are great for improving muscular tension when a child is placed facedown, arms stretched out in front of him, and rocked back and forth. You can also work on muscle control, positioning your child to lift his head or roll over on top of the ball while you roll the ball with him. If your child needs to develop a greater sense of balance, you can place her in a tailor-sit position on top of the ball, providing support where needed, and rock the ball or bounce her gently. Even my younger daughter who is not disabled loves these activities! Don't let the price hinder you from getting one of these balls. They may be expensive, but wouldn't it be best to put all of your child's

Christmas and birthday gift money from relatives into one fund? Then you may buy a great toy or enabling device that will be

beneficial and that your child will actually enjoy, rather than a lot of little toys she may never appreciate.

If your child is severely physically challenged, you may also want to look into equipment created by Rifton™ for *Project Move*. This is a fascinating program created to enable a child to develop skills necessary to be as physically independent as possible. Included in the equipment list are an adaptive chair, a mobile prone stander, and a gait trainer. These require some special training to use and are expensive, but many schools and facilities are beginning to provide the program and equipment for their children. The results have been astounding in many cases, so it is worth looking into with your child's educators.

Therapeutic equestrian riding for the disabled has been around for a long time and is increasing in popularity today. There are countless benefits to this type of program. It can serve to loosen muscular tone, maintain hip placement, increase balance, increase emotional bonding between the rider and the horse, as well as between the rider and trainer. Riding is the one thing that most closely parallels the natural motion of human walking. For this reason, it is used to train a child by patterning. Even if your child is severely disabled, a properly trained instructor can sit on the horse with your child to provide any necessary support. For more information about these programs, contact the North American Riding for the

Handicapped Association, Inc. (N.A.R.H.A.) at (800) 369-RIDE, or P.O. Box 33150, Denver, CO 80233. Not that you would find them at all comparable to the fine N.A.R.H.A. programs, but don't forget to take you child to the local pony rides. I have found that if I explain up front and ask special permission to walk beside the pony in order to provide support to my daughter, the owners are always very accommodating.

As mentioned, county fairs and theme parks are great sources of vestibular stimulation, if you dare go on the roller coasters and Ferris wheels with your child. Dana laughs for days after a trip to Disneyland, especially when I am driving with her in the car and get onto a freeway cloverleaf on-ramp!

Another way to get a similar sensation is to create a scooter board for your child with caster wheels and a rope tied to one end. You pull the rope and spin the board in circles while your child sits or lies down on it. (Instructions for scooter board are in Chapter Four.) Be careful to strap him on if his abilities deem it necessary, especially if he likes fast movements. Also, be careful that the child's fingers do not get pinched. In the winter months, the same activity can be done on the snow with a snowdisc or sled. What great family fun!

If family fun times attract you, what a joy it is to "rough house" and roll around together on the living room floor. Bounce your child on your feet while you lie on your back, legs curled above you. I have found this to be a great exercise for working on my daughter's balance. We do a lot of just moving together, too. I will move her arms in big circles while I sing songs. I walk with her feet on my own. We dance to all kinds of music, from waltzes to Mexican mariachi. I have to hold her in my arms or support her in a standing position, but she is very motivated by the music to move on her own.

There are so many things that you can do as a parent to help stimulate your child from early on to reach his maximum potential. I've offered a lot of ideas. Some of them may seem like great ideas to you. Some may not fit into your lifestyle very well. You may even feel a little overwhelmed with the pressure to perform. What if your child doesn't learn to manipulate play dough? Have you failed as a parent? Should you have taken more time to do that one extra exercise every day? Don't do that to yourself. The idea is to make this kind of activity just a natural part of your daily lives so that it doesn't become a chore or a source for guilt. You will do what is best for your child and yourself. Have fun with these activities. Keep it light and laugh. These are the joyous times that make up for the bad days.

And God Said "No"

— Claudia Minden Weisz

I asked God to take away my pride. God said, "NO."
It is not for me to take away, but for you to give it up.

I asked God to make my handicapped child whole.
God said, "NO." Her spirit is whole, her body is only temporary.

I asked God to grant me patience.
God said, "NO," patience is a by-product of tribulations, it isn't granted, it is earned.

I asked God to give me happiness.
God said, "NO." I give you blessings. Happiness is up to you.

I asked God to spare me pain.
God said, "NO." Suffering draws you apart from worldly cares and brings you closer to me.

I asked God to make my spirit grow.
God said, "NO." You must grow on your own, but I will prune you to make you fruitful.

I asked for all things that I might enjoy life.
God said, "NO." I will give you life so that you may enjoy all things.

I ask God to help me LOVE others, as much as he loves me.
God said. . .

Ahhhh, finally you have the idea.

4

FUN, INEXPENSIVE TOYS
EVEN YOU CAN MAKE AT HOME

*It's not what you lost, it's what you've got left
and what you do with it.*
— Franklin D. Roosevelt

Shopping for toys for one's child can be such a fun thing to do, but when you have a child with special needs it can be very frustrating and depressing. I dread having to do Christmas shopping for my daughter because it is so hard to find a toy that is appropriate for her abilities and age. Most toys usually require a good degree of strength and control, or they require sight, or they have obnoxious repetitive sounds that can drive any parent crazy! Actually, it is amazing how many wonderfully ingenious toys are on the market for children with special needs. There are many catalogs available with great ideas. The prices, however, can be daunting, presumably because there is such a small and specialized market for them.

I have found a few toys that can be made at home very easily and for a small fraction of the price. You need not even have much skill, just a willingness to be adventuresome. Some may seem so simple and yet can provide hours of entertainment for your child. Following are a few of the many ideas I have gotten from ingenious parents who were determined to find a way for their children to be able to play. After trying these, you will probably be inspired to try a few of your own!

PORTABLE TOY HANGER

This toy is wonderful for newborns on up. You can use it to hang interesting things to look at and touch. Even little ones that can't grasp can bat at the toys hanging in front of them. Put your child on the floor, and he can kick at toys that make sounds. Best yet, this toy is easy to make and breaks down to go with you wherever you go.

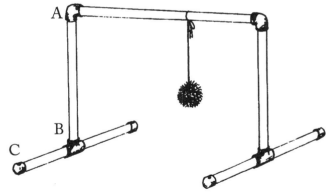

Materials, PVC pipe and fittings, ¾ inches diameter:
      one (1) piece 10 feet long
      two (2) elbows to connect top bar (A)
      two (2) T's to connect base (B)
      four (4) caps for base ends (C)

Directions:

Cut 10 foot piece of pipe into:

three (3) pieces 24 inches long

four (4) pieces 12 inches long

Assemble as in diagram.

Suspend toys, balloons, bells, or other items by elastic ties or ribbons

Portable Toy Hanger Activities:

Eyes —

The toy hanger is good to use as soon as your child starts looking up when lying on his back. Hang the toys right where the child is looking. Objects that will get his attention visually include: fancy bows from boxes, small colorful toys, white paper plates with simply drawn black designs, and foil covered toys.

NOTE: When your child can grab the dangling objects overhead, it is then time to replace the toys with ones that he can mouth safely (e.g., rattles, squeak toys, etc.).

Head And Shoulders —

Place a rolled towel or bolster under your child's upper chest. Encourage him to raise his head and shoulders by placing the toy hanger in front of him with a mirror underneath it. Draw his attention to the hanging toys as well as to his reflection in the mirror, encouraging him to push his head and shoulders up off of the floor.

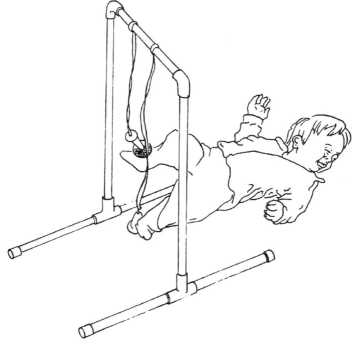

Ears —

Hang noisy objects such as bells, rattles, aluminum pie tins and metal measuring spoons. Hit the objects with a wooden spoon or a spatula. Watch to see if your child turns his head, trying to locate the different sounds.

Hands —

Help him to develop good eye-hand coordination by encouraging him to reach and grasp for objects with both hands. Hang interesting objects from the toy hanger within your child's reach. Gently guide his hands, showing him how to swat, grab, shake and manipulate objects. Suspend the toys using elastic ties so that he can bring the toys into his view for mouthing and exploration.

FEET —

Encourage your child to kick the toys that dangle from the toy hanger. Position the toy hanger above his feet while he is lying on his back. Also, let your child try this activity while lying on his tummy.

FEEL-Y QUILT

When you place your baby on the floor for a quiet time or for play time, why use just a flat, uninteresting, and un-stimulating blanket? Why not use this opportunity for a little added interest to his life? The "feel-y quilt" is a simple patchwork quilt using blocks of fabrics that offer a variety of textures, colors, and patterns. You'll need to be able to sew simple straight stitches, either by hand or with a machine, but even if you can't, I assure you that you will have no trouble finding someone who would love to make this for you.

Fabrics could be corduroy, velvet, heavy lace, satin, fur, flocked fabric, canvas, etc. Try to get the brightest colors possible to make it visually stimulating. Large black and white designs make an interesting effect, too. Don't go for beauty. Go for variety and stimulation. Scraps of fabric can be found almost anywhere. Ask friends, look at discarded clothing, or dig through piles at discount stores or swap meets.

Materials:

25 squares of different kinds of fabric, 8 x 10 inches
1½ yards Quilt batting
1½ yards fabric for backing (anything you like)
5 yards blanket binding
embroidery floss or yarn

Directions:

Cut your fabric pieces to a uniform size of 8 x 10 inches. This will allow for ⅜ inch seams.

Sew two squares together, right sides together, along one of the 8 inch sides.

Press seam open.

Sew another square in the same way to the unfinished 8 inch edge of one of the first two squares.

Press seam open.

Repeat until you have an 8 inch wide strip of five squares sewn end-to-end. **Sew other pieces together in the same way,** so that you will have five strips of five squares each.

Again, right sides together and using ⅜ inch seams, **sew two** strips together along one of the long edges. You will now have a block of ten squares, two by five. Do the same for the remaining strips until you have sewn all 25 pieces together into a block, five by five.

Press all seams flat.

Cut the batting to the same size as the quilt top and tack into place.

Cut the backing fabric to the same size and baste it along the edges to the batting and quilt top through all layers.

Baste blanket binding into place so that it wraps over the unfinished edges.

Miter at the corners and fold the end of the binding under to finish it when you have attached it all of the way around the quilt. **Sew into place.**

To keep batting from bunching up, tack at all of the corners where the quilt square pieces meet. Using a needle and yarn or embroidery floss, stitch through all layers as shown in the diagram below. Pull the loose ends until tight and tie them in a knot.

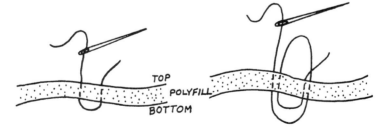

HOME MADE SCULPTING DOUGH

You could spend a fortune on commercial play dough, or you can have fun and make your own! Here is a great recipe for dough that has become a favorite among preschool teachers. It is very pliable and can last a long time when refrigerated. I like the way you can add flavored gelatin to make it a sensory experience for the nose, too!

Combine in a saucepan:
　1 cup flour
　½ cup salt
　2 teaspoons cream of tartar

Mix in measuring cup:
　1 cup water
　1 tablespoon oil
　1 teaspoon food coloring

Gradually stir liquid into dry ingredients.

When mixture is smooth, cook over medium heat, stirring constantly until a ball forms.

Remove from heat.

Add 2 tablespoons of a coordinated color of sugar free flavored gelatin and knead until smooth.

The gelatin adds rich scents to the dough.

Plate Switch

One of the best inventions ever has been the adaptive switch. It comes in many shapes and sizes, depending on the needs of the individual who will be using it. Some examples were discussed in a previous chapter. These switches are simply terrific because they can open up whole new worlds for our special children. A child who once had no control of his environment can now, with a simple movement of a finger or other part of his body, make a battery-operated toy come to life! He can help make breakfast by turning on a battery-operated mixer. He can communicate his wants and needs. He can make choices for himself. All he needs is an appropriate switch and a connection between the switch and the battery-operated device. The switch plugs into one end

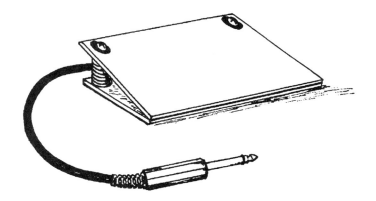

of the adapter/connection and the other end goes between the batteries and their terminals. No problem. Except, each adapter costs about $15.00 to $20.00. You can make them for about $2.00. You'll find all of the parts you need at any electronics store and, with a little practice, you will start putting these together like an assembly line. It's that easy. What new worlds will this open up for your little one?

Materials:

piece of wood cut to desired size
piece of Masonite or Plexiglas™ the same size as the
  wood
4-5 feet of two-conductor wire (22 or 24 gauge)
2 wood screws
one small brass wood screw
washers
small piece of copper/brass
small piece of foam/spring
phone plug (male)

Directions:

Prepare plywood, Masonite or Plexiglas™; drill holes for
screws as shown in diagrams.

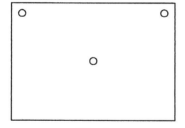
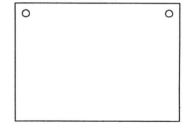

Wood   *Masonite or Plexiglass™*

Split a two-conductor wire approximately ½ inch on one end,
and 2 inches on the other.

Strip off ½ inch of the plastic coating on each of the four
ends.

Solder one wire (from end split 2 inches) to the small piece of
copper/brass and attach the other to the brass screw in
the piece of wood, being careful not to break the wire

when installing the screw.

Glue the copper/brass sheet onto the under side of the Masonite or Plexiglas™ just above the brass screw so that contact will be made when the switch is activated.

Assemble wood base and Masonite or Plexiglas™ with two wood screws. Adjust the height of the Masonite or Plexiglas™ with washers until desired height is obtained.

Solder remaining wires to the phone plug, and plug into an adapted toy or toy adapter.

Place piece of foam/spring near brass screw and experiment with placement until desired switch operation is obtained. The closer the foam/spring is to the screw, the more pressure is required to operate the switch.

Tips For Successful Soldering:

1. Be sure items to be soldered are clean. If not, use a small piece of steel wool or sandpaper to clean the surfaces.

2. Briefly hold the soldering iron against the wire and the surface the wire is being soldered to (to heat the connections).

3. Hold the solder on the connections just in front of the soldering iron tip. The solder should melt and flow onto the surfaces.

4. Remove the solder and the iron and allow the joint to cool and the solder to harden.

5. The wire should be stabilized during the entire process (with pliers or masking tape if necessary).

Toy Adapter
(to be used with adaptive switch)

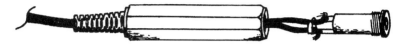

Materials:

1 three-conductor phone jack
12 inches of speaker wire
electrician's tape
2 small thin sheets copper or brass
small piece thin cardboard
solder
glue

Directions:

Unscrew cap from jack and slide it onto the wire.

Split wire approximately 2 inches and strip off ½ inch of the plastic coating from each end.

Thread wire through holes in metal prongs of the jack as shown in diagram, from the inside toward the outside.

Bend and wrap wire against itself, making sure there are no stray strands.

Solder each **wire** with a tiny amount of solder and wrap a small piece of electrician's tape around the small prong.

Screw the **cap** on.

Split the **wire** on opposite end approximately 2 inches and strip ½ inch off each end.

Cut a circle of cardboard the diameter of the negative end of the battery.

Cut two circles of copper/brass slightly smaller than the cardboard circle.

Heat a wire and one piece of the copper/brass with soldering iron.

Add the solder to connect the surfaces and stabilize until cool.

Repeat the process with the other half of the wire and the second piece of copper/brass.

Use a small amount of glue to attach the cardboard circle between the two copper/brass circles.

Insert this end between the battery and its metal contact inside the battery compartment of your child's toy. You may want to file a slot in the battery compartment cover in order to make room for the wire.

Plug the male jack of the plate switch into the female end of the adapter.

LIGHTED HAPPY FACE

This is a great toy to use with your new plate switch and adapter. Again, it uses very basic electronics. If you need any help, the salesperson at your local electronics store will probably love to help out. Your little one will love to interact with this bright, smiling face.

Materials:

one box
two small clear plastic bottles or cups
one 2 "C" cell battery holder
two "C" batteries
three bulbs with sockets and wire
      (miniature Christmas tree lights
one piece of wire 6-7 inches long
one miniature phone jack
small sheet of cellophane
solder
hot melt glue gun and glue

Directions:

Strip ¼ inch of **plastic** coating from each of the Christmas light wires and from each end of the 6-7 inch wire.

Plan face on box and cut out areas for bottle eyes, nose and mouth.

Glue bases of light bulb sockets to openings of small plastic bottles with hot melt glue.

Glue cellophane over openings of nose and mouth inside box and glue eyes in place. **Position and glue** third bulb in place so that the light will shine through the cellophane.

Take one **wire** from each of the sockets, **twist** ends together and **solder** to one of the terminals of the miniature jack. **Twist the other three wires** together **and solder** to one of the wires on the battery holder. Solder one end of the 6-7 inch wire to the second terminal of the miniature jack and the other end to the second wire on the battery holder.

Mount the jack on the side of the box by making a small hole with a sharp pointed tool.

Glue the battery holder to the side of the box to stabilize it.

LIGHT BOX

Professionals in the field of infant stimulation often rely on the use of a large lighted apparatus that looks something like the lighted backgrounds that doctors use to read X-rays. It is great for visual stimulation. The children can get right up close and

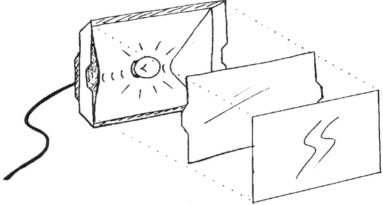

interact with shapes, colors and patterns that are a little easier to see because of the stimulus of a lighted source. It's a great idea and kids just seem to love it! The problem is that these commercial "light boxes" cost hundreds of dollars, so only the most affluent of early childhood stimulation programs can afford to make them available. That pretty much leaves most parents out of being able to put one under the Christmas tree for our sons and daughters. It provides such a wonderful opportunity for stimulating interaction, though. Call me cheap, but I figured there had to be another way. This simple design works just fine. I have yet to find any child with even the smallest amount of vision that hasn't been enchanted by the light and colors from this toy.

Materials:

Light Bright™ Toy
1 sheet of translucent plastic ¹/₁₆- ¼ inch thick
25 watt bulb
acetate sheets for overhead projectors
black construction paper

Directions:

Have plastic sheet cut to the same shape as black peg board of Light Bright or, using a utility knife, graze outline and carefully snap away edges.

Assemble Light Bright™ as indicated in diagram, replacing black peg board with translucent plastic

Place acetate sheets on light board for visually stimulating activities. Acetate may be purchased in different colors or clear.

Light Box Activities:

● **Cut a 3-inch square shape** out of the center of a piece of construction paper and place it on the light box. Have your child reach for the square. This may be done with different shapes to teach shape recognition. As your child becomes more skilled at this activity, cut smaller shapes or cut shapes at sides or corners of the paper and ask him to locate and touch them. Place colored acetate under the paper to make shapes different colors.

● **Cut a sideways 'S' shape** out of the construction paper. Place paper on light box and slowly slide a piece of colored acetate under the paper. The color will appear to move along the "snake."

- **Glue different shapes and patterns** cut from construction paper onto the acetate to create visually stimulating contrasting designs for your child to look at and touch.

- **Place favorite toys or blocks** on the light box and ask your child to reach out and pick them up. Again, the light creates a contrast.

SCOOTER BOARD

All kids can benefit from crawling around. It is very interesting that some studies have shown that the amount of time a child spends crawling on the floor during infancy can greatly affect other more advanced skills in the future, such as reading and sequencing. Some of our kids just do not have the strength or balance to be able to crawl. That is why some brilliant person came up with the idea of a board on wheels to help support the child while he pushes himself along. I do not know who that person

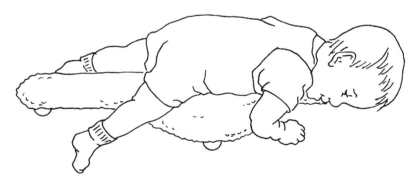

was, but the concept came out on the commercial market as the Crawligator™. It was a green plastic alligator-shaped toy molded to fit the contours of an infant's body. An infant could lie on her tummy and use her arms and legs to scoot around. The Crawligator™ also retailed for over $50.00, but you can make an inexpensive imitation using scrap lumber that basically will do the same thing. The most expensive parts are the casters which you can find at any good hardware store.

Materials:

one small sheet of ¾ inch plywood, cut into the desired shape (see following illustration for an example)

sandpaper

glue

one piece of foam rubber scrap, 1-2 inches thick and big enough to cover the entire plywood shape plus 1 inch all the way around.

approximately 1 yard of sheepskin fabric or vinyl (according to desires) and big enough to cover entire plywood shape plus 3 inches all the way around.

four **high-quality** casters

staple gun and staples

screw driver

Directions:

Using a jig saw or small handsaw, cut plywood into desired shape.

Sand any rough edges or splinters.

Glue the foam rubber onto the board with one inch extending beyond all sides.

Lay the board, foam-side down, onto the wrong side of the fabric with three inches of fabric extending on all sides.

Gently pull the fabric around the edge of the board and **staple**

into place. Do the same on the opposite side of the scooter board. Slowly work your way around the board, stapling as you go and clipping or tucking curves as necessary, until the entire board is upholstered with the fabric.

Screw casters into place on the bottom or wood side of the board, according to the Xs on the diagram.

Optional: You may wish to drill a large hole at the top of the board and tie a pull rope through the hole to provide another type of activity.

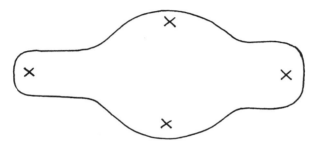

Caution: Use only with parental supervision.

How To Bake A Cake

— Mikey's Funnies,
www.youthspecialties.com/mikeysfunnies

Preheat oven, get out utensils and ingredients.

Remove blocks and toy cars from table.

Grease pan, crack nuts.

Measure two cups flour.

Remove baby's hands from flour, wash flour off baby.

Re-measure flour.

Put flour, baking powder, salt in sifter.

Get dustpan and brush up pieces of bowl baby
knocked on floor.

Get another bowl.

Answer doorbell.

Return to kitchen.

Remove baby's hands from bowl.

Wash baby.

Answer phone.

Return.

Remove 1/4 inch salt from greased pan.

Look for baby.

Grease another pan.

Answer telephone.

Return to kitchen and find baby.

Remove baby's hands from bowl.

Take up greased pan, find layer of nutshells in it.

Head for baby, who flees, knocking bowl off table.

Wash kitchen floor, table, wall, dishes.

Call baker.

Lie down.

5

ENCOURAGING
VERBAL AND NON-VERBAL COMMUNICATION

Victory is not won in miles but in inches.
Win a little now, hold your ground,
and later win some more.
— Louis L'amour

If we want to instill independence in our children and to nurture loving and close relationships, then we must take steps to encourage communication as much as possible. Communication is the most essential element in being able to have some control over one's life. We all need communication to make our own choices. It helps us develop dignity, self-esteem, and interpersonal relationships. This chapter covers a few suggestions for parents who wish to help their children in these areas.

Talk about everything! Talk especially about those things your child experiences directly. In other words, if your child is visually impaired, don't start out by trying to describe colors. Not that the subject is taboo for children with vision problems. It just does not help to encourage communication in those circumstances.

Instead, talk about how warm is their bath water, how loud is the train whistle, how sweet is the apple sauce, how smooth is the big rubber ball, and "don't those cookies smell great?" If your child is hearing impaired, you'll still want to talk to her all of the time. Make sure you have her attention and her eyes are on you. Then, speak clearly. She will see how your face and mouth move. Let her touch your lips and throat to feel the vibrations.

Do yourself and your child a big favor and **learn sign language.** Begin to use it immediately. Remember, most disabilities separate people from things and places, but an inability to communicate separates people from other people. Teach your child as many ways to communicate as possible. My husband and I took a sign language class when our younger daughter was just an infant. We would practice together at home to prepare for the next class. To our amazement, our infant began using some of the signs. She was using sign language before speaking her first words! Children seem to pick it up so easily. Sign language is not just for the deaf. It has also been used very successfully with people with Down's syndrome, developmental delays and cerebral palsy.

Read. Begin reading to your child from the day she is born. Just the sound of your voice can be soothing and calming or stimulating and exciting. Reading gives you the opportunity to introduce your child to new words, sounds and emotions. Children's poems are good because, as the popularity of Dr. Suess and Mother Goose has proven, children are very attracted to rhyming sounds.

Music is also very engaging to children, so **singing can be a wonderful way to stimulate language skills.** Many children's songs offer opportunities to add hand movements or sign language. Why not use all of the tools available to you to teach your child different ways to communicate?.

Offer many different tactual experiences, such as feet in a bowl of dried rice, or hands in some peanut butter or sand. Try tickling his tummy with a feather. All of these experiences not only stimulate your child in physical ways, but offer opportunities to talk about his experiences.

It may seem strange, but **eating has a lot to do with developing verbal skills.** It takes a great deal of oral dexterity to be able to eat some foods. If at all possible, do not allow your child to eat puréed baby food all her life. Continue to offer different textures so she can acquire the skills necessary to move her mouth and tongue appropriately for speech.

Have your child lie down next to you with his head on your arm so you are very close and face-to-face with one of his arms free to move. **Guide him to touch your lips as you speak or make sounds.** Repeat any sound he makes. Show great pleasure any time he makes a sound. As your child begins to show some control over what sounds he makes, try to get him to mimic sounds you make and praise him when he does. Start with sounds your child may already be able to utter. Don't forget the all-important vowel sounds and the funny faces you can make when you say them!

When playing these sound games with Dana, I began with throaty sounds like "G" and "K" because those are sounds she seemed to have some control of already. Then, we moved on to sounds made with the lips, such as "B," "M," "P," "V," and raspberries. Next, we moved on to sounds made with the tongue that were even a little harder for her, sounds like "D" and "N." Your child may have abilities with other sounds. The important thing to do is just to start where his abilities lie, and slowly add to them. Have fun with this, and be patient. It may be a slow process, but the rewards are well worth the effort.

Be very encouraging, accepting whatever verbalization your child uses to try to communicate throughout the day. Then, with a smile, offer her the correct, or accepted pronunciation.

When Dana was very young, the school "specialists" wanted to push Dana heavily into technological devices for communication. Since she did seem to have an ability to use a plate switch, technology was the chosen path for communication. I had my doubts, however, about her ability to convert concrete objects or needs to the symbolic thought needed to use technology in communicating. I gently protested, pointing out that it was hardly logical to give up on spoken communication at her young age. I was well aware that children learn new skills by building on what they already know. Why could we not use sounds she could already make and assign meaning to them? Thus we would create her own sort of language. We made a list of the sounds Dana could make on command and decided that a "cough" was the best sound to mean "yes." We would eventually work that sound into more of a "yeah" sound, which is an acceptable affirmative response in the community. "Uh" would mean "no," working that into "uh-uh." Again, this is acceptable and understood by almost everyone. I knew if we could just get a clear "yes" and "no," important communication could, for the first time, become a part of our lives together. The school agreed to try.

Our ideas worked, and we now have a way to allow our child to make clear choices in her life at any moment. We don't have to drag out some electronic device so she can hit the proper switch. We do, however use communication devices to supplement the "yes" and "no." I think they are marvelous in certain circumstances, like making a choice between chocolate milk and juice, and there is certainly a wide array of devices to choose from. They are easily ordered from special equipment catalogs. Still, the ease of having some form of verbal (or in some cases, physical) "yes" and "no" is irreplaceable. The trick is to find the child's strengths and build on them. That may mean using eye movements, sign language, foot extension, facial expressions, or whatever else could creatively be made into communication in order to facilitate an expression of needs or feelings.

Please know that there are many developmental theories that describe the progressive steps in developing speech. Most claim that nouns (people, places and things such as "Mama," "out," and "ball") come first, then verbs, then adjectives, etc. This would be the development of language in a normal child. However, I believe there needs to be room for exceptions in the language development of a child with physical limitations. The cognitive understanding of words may develop in the same way, but the ability to verbalize certain verbs may come before common nouns. In other words, do not limit your child's abilities just because he has not conquered verbalizing simple nouns. This is also true of a blind child whose world of experience may be more limited to physical actions than to contact with other objects in the environment.

No matter what grammatical or physical form the communication is taking, it is of utmost importance to remember that the development of communication must be a logical progression of abilities. For instance, if a plate switch of some kind is to be the preferred form of communication, then your child must first be able to extend his arm. Then he must be able to target a spot and touch it. Next, he needs to have a switch available to suite his abilities, like a large plate switch, or a smaller "Jelly Bean" switch. If your child needs to use a sip and puff switch with his mouth, then it follows that first you will need to break down the steps needed, including working on head control, the ability to complete lip closure around an object, etc. Little steps, one at a time, will reduce frustration and get results.

My Perfect Child

— Joyce Martin

*As my children were born, I wanted them to be perfect.
When they were babies, I wanted them to smile and to be content
playing with their toys. I wanted them to be happy and to laugh
continually instead of crying and being demanding. I wanted them
to see the beautiful side of life.*

*As they grew older, I wanted them to be giving instead of
selfish. I wanted them to skip the terrible twos.
I wanted them to stay innocent forever.*

*As they became teenagers, I wanted them to be obedient and
not rebellious, mannerly and not mouthy.
I wanted them to be full of love, gentle and kindhearted.*

*"Oh, God, give me a child like this," was often my prayer.
One day he did! Some called him handicapped. . .
I called him perfect! His name is Troy Anthony!*

—IN LOVING MEMORY OF OUR SON, BROTHER,
UNCLE, NEPHEW, BROTHER-IN-LAW AND FRIEND,
TROY ANTHONY MARTIN (2/8/78—4/5/93).

6

GETTING THE BEST
CARE AND EDUCATION FOR YOUR CHILD

Joy is the oil that reduces the friction of life.
— unknown

One of the greatest challenges facing you as an exceptional parent is getting appropriate services and help for your child. In many cases, parents must become well educated in medical practices and terminology, as well as become a sort of legal rights defender. You, as the parent, are the person most acquainted with your child's needs. In most cases, it will be up to you to fight for appropriate services. This may seem a little intimidating at first, but it soon becomes such a common occurrence that you will begin to wonder what you'll be fighting for next. I do not mean to sound negative or militant. This is all just a part of our lives as parents of special kids. There are many services available, but parents must learn to find those services. Regulations and laws are there to help our kids, but we must know them and acquire the skills to help ourselves. The experiences of other parents who have been successful should be useful to you.

INFORMATION BOOK

Before you begin advocating for your child, you should make yourself well prepared. Your life gets so swallowed up with appointments and home programs that it is easy to become unorganized and loose track of important details. I have found it helpful that at the very outset I created a binder to hold all pertinent information relating to Dana. It is a binder I can take with me wherever we go, be it to the doctor, school, or social service organization.

Following is a list of what I included for my own use. You may want to modify my ideas to suit your own special circumstances:

- Information about organizations that may be helpful in providing knowledge, services, financial help, and support.

- Home programs and evaluations given to me by the various occupational and physical therapists.

- A list of medications and doses.

- Copies of insurance cards and coverage information.

- Personal information about Dana that can be handed to professionals to help them know how she communicates and how best to communicate to her. For instance, I include information on how to give a shot to a child who is blind.

- Items representing Dana's history and development, including photos that demonstrate her learned abilities, report cards, notes from teachers, immunization records, newspaper clippings, birth records, apgar scores, etc.

- Notes from speaking engagements so that I can refer to them if asked to speak about a subject more than once.

- A list of phone numbers: doctors, specialists, caseworkers, respite care, supportive people.

- Contacts and correspondences with other parents in similar situations.

- All correspondence with researching staff.

- All evaluations of my daughter's development and reports from specialists (hearing tests, eye exams, social-development tests, speech and language assessments, etc.). I divide this by subject or doctor's specialty.

- Copies of all of Dana's Individualized Education Plans (I.E.P.s).

- Binder paper for taking notes.

- Information from support group meetings.

- Lastly, but most importantly, I include clippings of articles, poems, sayings and short essays that give me a boost.

I wrap all of this together into a colorful binder with my daughter's name boldly written on the front and spine, and I make sure it has a prominent place on the book shelf so I can easily find it to access its information. I am sure you will find, as I have, how valuable it is to have this information in one place where it is easily available. I am constantly using the information within it to update doctors and specialists on Dana's progress or condition. I use it as my reference book during an I.E.P. meeting. I use it as a place to put records that would otherwise become lost so easily.

I have a confession to make, however. After eight years I have too many reports and evaluations to store in a single binder. I began to file the old ones and keep only the more recent and pertinent papers in the book. That way, the old records are still organized and accessible, but I do not have to carry fifty pounds of paperwork everywhere I go. It is a good idea to summarize some of the documents that have been filed so that the most pertinent information stays with you in the binder. An example of this would be a list of past surgeries and dates. Another would be the bottom line of test results, including the name of the test given and the date. Everybody always seems to want to know what has been done before and what was the outcome. It will take a little time, but you will soon learn which information and files are frivolous and which are essential to keep with you for your individual child's needs.

HOSPITALIZATIONS

Any parent faces the possibility of a child having to spend time in a hospital. We, as parents of children with disabilities, are almost sure to spend many hours at a bedside. My own daughter is actually one of the more fortunate. I think we have averaged only one major surgery per year, not counting the hospitalizations for bronchial asthma and respiratory infections. Hospital staff members who have come to know us have jokingly offered us frequent flyer benefits! After the first few experiences, it became clear that there are a few simple things to consider in order to make a hospital visit as comfortable as possible for both our children and us parents. First and foremost, it is imperative that we come prepared. Outside the usual things to bring to the hospital (change of clothes, necessary medications, etc.) I have found it helpful to include a few extras when I know Dana will be in for an extended stay. This is assuming, of course, that the hospital graciously allows me to stay with Dana and sleep on one of those unaccommodating, bumpy vinyl lounge chairs.

I always bring a printed sheet with brief instructions for nurses and doctors regarding the care of children with visual impairments, and I tape it up in clear sight. This includes instructions to speak naturally, call the child by name, explain what is happening, use words instead of gestures, tell them when a prick is coming, etc. You may wish to have information about children with hearing impairments, or cerebral palsy. Maybe it is important for you to list medications, or allergies, or specific doctor's instructions, depending on your circumstances and your child. I even keep Dana's instruction sheet on file on my home computer so I can print a copy anytime. I also, as mentioned, make sure I have one in my information book. Another pointer is to make it colorful and attractive and highlight the most important information. It is more likely to catch the caregiver's eye that way.

Make it so the staff will want to read it. Draw balloons or smiley faces on it if you have to: whatever it takes to make people read it and receive the information. Review the instructions with each shift of nursing staff. Different shifts do not have much time to communicate much between themselves, so you must make it your responsibility to make sure they understand what your individual child needs. Preferably, you will be at your child's side to advocate or instruct, but if for some reason you cannot be there, or if you have to step away for a few minutes, you can rest in the fact that the information that needs to get across will be there on the page you created. Hospital staff members have often mentioned how much it helps.

If you have the opportunity, be sure to bring toys. This seems like a "no-brainer," but it just kills me how often I see little ones banging their feet on the railings of their crib because they have nothing else to keep themselves entertained. A familiar and favorite "old friend" can comfort your child and help with his boredom. If you do not have a chance to bring something from home, many hospitals have resource rooms that will let you borrow toys or books. Even just a bright balloon, for some reason I do not fully comprehend, can keep an ill child's attention for hours! As a side note, be aware that some hospitals seem to prefer toys without fur or fuzz.

Tape recorders are another great way to help make the hours pass. Dana has often been comforted or entertained by tapes of favorite music and stories. Caring and thoughtful friends and classmates have recorded messages that bring smiles. This is a fabulous idea for letting siblings help to keep in touch and care for their brother or sister. After all, their world gets tuned upside-down, too, when there is a hospitalization. They can feel comforted and important by an opportunity to help out in some way.

As for you, the parent, you'll need ways to keep your sanity, too. May I recommend that you take up needlework? Seriously, don't forget to bring a good book or a project to work on while you wait. I read a lot of stories aloud to my daughter; it helps to keep her mind off of the surroundings, and it is a great comfort to her to hear my voice nearby. Then, I do more needlework! My mind is usually too occupied to concentrate on a book.

If you haven't had enough time to prepare it beforehand, have someone from home bring you a bag packed with candy bars, a blanket and/or pillow, coins and bills or credit cards for vending machines and phone calls, and a toothbrush for yourself. Bring comfortable clothing because you will most likely be sleeping in it — possibly for days! Lastly, do not forget to bring along your child's information book and some paper to jot down any instructions from the doctor. You will be exhausted and may not be able to remember well all of the details. Did I mention needlework?

Advocacy In Medical Care

It is understood that not everyone has access to the best medical care in the country, but all of us can have some control over the quality of medical care our child receives. When Dana was diagnosed with congenital toxoplasmosis, I was informed of Dr. McLeod's research in Chicago. I was given information regarding the research program requirements, and I made an appointment with a local infectious disease specialist. I sat in the specialist's office, ready to discuss the regimen. She solemnly reviewed the material, shook her head and informed me that she didn't have time for such a thing and that if I really looked at the schedule requirements, I wouldn't want to do it either. That was the first time I realized that it was okay to disagree with a doctor, excuse myself, and continue searching for one who would be wiling to give his or her time to my daughter's well-being. I have left the offices of more than one doctor, vowing never to return. I am

What to Take to the Hospital:

- ☐ Insurance card(s)
- ☐ Information Sheet
- ☐ Information Book
- ☐ Note Paper and Pens
- ☐ Comfort Toys
- ☐ Tape Recorder
- ☐ Toothbrush, hair brush, razor
- ☐ Snacks and bottled water
- ☐ Coins and Credit Cards
- ☐ Comfortable change of clothes
- ☐ Medications
- ☐ Books and needlework

not looking for a miracle cure. I have simply decided that those who regard Dana as an individual and believe in her abilities to continue to learn and develop will give her the best medical care. They are the ones who understand that she is *part* of the family, not the center of it, and they believe that it is possible for Dana and her family members to lead a full and happy life, in spite of her multiple disabilities.

One thing that quickly becomes apparent is that doctors are merely human. With all due respect, they are after all, just regular folk who have education in the medical field. Only a very few think they are God! Many have become my good friends. Almost all are in the profession because they really want to help. I have even come into contact with some who were obviously uncomfortable around my daughter and me because they knew they didn't have the answers and couldn't "fix it" for us. Bless them. In all of their efforts to help, many have sent me on proverbial wild goose chases by referring me over to one specialist after another, hoping the next person would have better answers.

Sometimes this can be a real problem. More than once we have been prepared for a major procedure to be performed by one doctor who assumed that another doctor had prescribed it. In reality, all the first doctor wanted was a second opinion! Somehow, the lines of communication can break down.

Just the other day we found ourselves in an orthotist's office being fitted for new ankle-foot orthotics (those plastic braces that

fit around the ankle). The gentleman was going into great detail
about how he was going to change the design and create a new
type of pad that Dana could wear to help prevent breakdown of
her ankle tissue. I finally started asking a few questions. In my
perception, no one had yet even looked to see if the orthotics that
Dana already had still fit her! No one had told me why they were
not working properly for her any more. No one had explained to
me adequately just exactly where the problem was and why we
needed all new orthotics. I thought we were just there for this
guy to take a quick look at what she had and tell us they were still
fine for her. As it turned out, I am glad I asked. He looked at me
very sheepishly and admitted that he had just jumped in on an
assumption that the doctor who had referred us to him had done
a thorough examination of the ankles and the orthotics. When
he took a closer look and actually tried the braces on Dana's feet,
he realized that they were indeed quite functional for her. We
thanked him very much and went on our way.

The lesson here is, never assume anything! Never just blindly go
along for the ride, thinking that the doctor must know what's
best because he is the doctor! I am not saying that you should not
have faith in the medical profession. To the contrary. I am just
giving you, as the parent, as the expert in your child, the freedom
to ask questions. You are the glue that holds all of the various
doctors and medical treatments together. You are the constant
that runs throughout the entire process. Pay very close attention
to all that doctors have to say. Ask all of your questions. Be sure
you understand exactly what is being planned for the treatment

of your little one and exactly why your child needs it. How will it help? What are the risks? What is the expected outcome? What is the chance it will work? Who will be doing it, and what are his or her qualifications? What are the alternatives? Make sure you are comfortable and confident about what is being offered or provided for your child.

If your hospital or medical staff cannot provide the services you think are necessary and appropriate, ask them who can. You may wish to go to a university library to find out who is on the leading edge of medicine for your child's disorder. You can then call their offices and inquire about help for your child. Keep searching until you find what is clearly best for your child. I only have one caution. What is best for your child may not necessarily be flying him or her to all corners of the earth in search of a cure. Remember that a warm and secure home life may be better medicine. Then again, in some cases, travel may be necessary and best. As stated before, only you are the specialist for your child's needs.

You may find at some point that your problems in getting appropriate medical care may not lie in your physicians or facilities, but rather in your medical insurance. With the costs of medical care on such a dramatic increase, insurance agencies are really cutting back on benefits. If there is ever any question whether or not a procedure or piece of equipment is covered, it is usually denied. You do not have to just accept a "no" answer, however. There are ways in which you can contest the decision. If you are being denied coverage over the phone, politely ask to speak to the supervisor. If they also deny your child the coverage you seek, find out from them what you need to do on your part to get it. You may be asked to provide letters written by the doctors involved, stating the need for the prescribed treatment. If you have done all they ask and you are still being denied coverage that you feel your child should be eligible to receive, you can ask that the case be taken to arbitration.

Insurance companies have review boards made up of doctors and nurses that look over the records and the requests being arbitrated. They make judgements based on what they read. The big problem for you is that the insurance companies usually are the ones who hire these boards of review. Not to cause alarm, but this is a big machine. If your experience takes you to the table like this, do not try it alone. There are organizations, both for-profit and not-for-profit, who specialize in helping parents advocate for their children's medical needs. These are professionals who do this for a living. Take full advantage of their expertise. Just a few phone calls can help you to find out what organizations exist in your area that can help you advocate for medical services for your child.

ADVOCACY IN EDUCATION

I find that most exceptional parents have the greatest respect for the educators of our children. I am one of those parents. These teachers have devoted their own lives to making better lives for our children. They have no personal stake in the betterment of their students, and yet they put in painstaking hours and efforts to gain little advances. The majority of them rank among the saints in my mind. However, there are times when a parent may need to fight the educational system in order to get what they know their child needs. These are the times when one has to tighten one's bootstraps and prepare to be disappointed, disillusioned, and angry. There are so many laws and regulations in the education system, especially in regard to funding. No one wants to end up spending money for services for a child that could be covered by other service organizations or school districts. An awful lot of finger pointing goes on. In addition, boundaries between districts or S.E.L.P.A.s (Special Education Local Plan Areas) are very clearly drawn. They are almost impossible to cross. You may find yourself living within a mile of a marvelous program that seems most appropriate for your child without the ability to access it because it is in a different district or S.E.L.P.A. In some instances, it may even be worth a move! Your child has a right to an appropriate education in the least restrictive environment.

In the very worst of cases, school officials have been known to lie about what is available in your district. Sometimes there is complete disregard for regulations that have been set up for the protection of your child. Sometimes the district officials ignore the statutes that set out exactly what must be provided. The excuse is almost always funding problems. This paints a terrible picture that is not necessarily the norm, but it also underscores the importance of being prepared, professional, and well informed so that there is no chance that your child may be cheated of his rights.

The greatest force in advocacy for your child's education is advanced preparation for the Individualized Education Plan (I.E.P.) meeting. This is a gathering of the special education department personnel in your school district, school psychologists, physical therapists, occupational therapists, speech therapists, mobility and orientation instructors, visual stimulation specialists, behavioral therapists, teachers, principals, social workers, advocates, family, friends, and anyone else who may be involved in or can advocate for your child's special education needs. Everyone sits around a big table and decides how best to fill your child's individual education needs in order to help him reach his greatest potential. This sounds daunting, does it not? A lot of parents like to make you think it will be the worst experience in your life! I think they're just trying to make an impression. It really does not need to be all that bad. All of these "specialists" are just regular people that happen to be a part of your little one's education. You are the expert. They are there to serve you and your child. This is your opportunity to ask for the benefits that you believe your child should have.

Parents ought to be as well informed and professional as the teaching staff if they want to be taken seriously. You will need to know what your child has already accomplished, what he is capable of doing in the near future, and what you would like to strive for in the long term. Write a list clearly stating at least three major short-term goals for your child's education. Then decide what steps you would like to see taken to achieve those goals. Lastly, make a note of what you can do at home to support what the teaching staff is doing in these areas. If you have trouble with how to accomplish the goals, don't fret. That is why the teaching staff is there. They are trained to know how to break goals down into teachable steps. You do need to make sure, however, that when goals and techniques are written into the I.E.P. they are written clearly and measurably. An example would be "Joey will be able to sit in tailor-sit position for thirty seconds with no assistance three out of five times by September 1, such-and-such year." You are not required to sign your approval of an I.E.P. unless you are in complete agreement with it, and you may revoke your approval at any time. It should not be this way, but reality dictates that you the parent need to make sure that the teaching staff carries through on what has been written into an I.E.P. Otherwise, they are "out of compliance," three words the educational system hates to hear. This may be due to incompetence, but usually seems to be due to some oversight. Consider yourself the case manager and check up occasionally on how the work of the staff is complying with your child's education plan.

Maintain calm and professionalism at all times, and the staff will be more willing to work with you instead of against you. Understand that they are working with time constraints, limited staffing and budgets. I only say this because I have known parents who had made outrageous demands of the school district that could have caused my daughter's school extreme financial hardship. Nevertheless, plainly make your requirements known. Your child will probably not receive all that is available to him unless you ask. It is important to keep informed of what programs and services are possible. You can gather information at parent workshops or support groups. Interaction with other parents is very helpful. Also, keep well read on the issues regarding your child's disability. You may be able to share information and ideas with officials in the school district or at the school site. They are on the "front lines" of special education and may also know about new trends that may benefit your son or daughter. You may learn of something else that is available of which neither you nor your child's school were aware. It may be even something that will spark new programs to benefit many children in your area. Most importantly in your role as your child's advocate, get your hands on the State Regulations for Special Education in your state. You can get a copy from the special education department in your school district. You need to read them and know them so that you can catch any errors made by the school officials, whether they are intentional or not.

What if you are afraid of enrolling your child in a special education program for fear of labeling her in a way that might be harmful in the future? In some instances, I am sure there is some reason for concern, but do not let that keep you from using whatever tools are available to you for getting the best education for your child. There is a very strong push right now for full inclusion, in lieu of segregated special education classes. This means placing children of all levels of ability into age-defined classes. For instance, a seven-year-old child would be placed in a regular second grade class along with other seven-year-olds, regardless of her developmental level. This even includes those children with severe developmental delay. It supposedly helps do away with labeling or discrimination due to disability. The theory behind this approach is that those children with significant disabilities benefit from the challenge of interacting with their peers. The regular education children benefit from an increased acceptance of other's differences. There are many special children who show potential for being able to live independent lives in the future. It would obviously be helpful to give them experiences in ordinary surroundings. I know of quite a few families who have opted for this approach to their child's education, and they seem pretty pleased with the results, so it can work well.

We must remember, though, that every child has different and individual needs. Those who lobby for full inclusion for every child are taking their argument a bit too far. In reality, full inclusion seems to be successful with only a small percentage of children. For a child like my daughter, Dana, the program seems unsuitable. The school district would have to provide a person in the class just to move her, feed her, and take care of her hygienic needs. The school would have to provide an appropriate, private place in which to do so. The other children in the class would have to put up with the disruption of Dana screaming at inappropriate moments, which she does quite often. My daughter would have to sit through lessons on memorization of addition tables when she presently shows no ability to recognize the concept of numbers. What she really needs to learn is how to grasp and release objects, how to communicate her preferences, and how to sit patiently while her mother is standing in line at the check-out counter. Yes, she would have a full-time aid to work with her privately during such times, but how interactive is that? She would be losing out on the benefits that the full-inclusion programs promise. I would not put her or the other children of her age through the trauma of a full inclusion program.

I have heard, read, and conducted interviews with children who are blind, deaf or mildly delayed, and it is interesting that all of them showed a preference for special education. They claim it provides an environment in which they are comfortable being with children who face similar challenges. It is a place where they do not feel like a freak around the other children. Then again, there is a happy medium when you can have a little of both worlds. This is what seems to work best for our family and for Dana. She has the benefit of education that is appropriate for her needs and is with other children with whom she can relate. At the same time, she has the opportunity to interact with her regular education peers at times when the activities seem conducive to interaction, such as lunch, story time, recess, music and art.

In short, do not steer away from special education just because it might "label" your child. If that is what it takes to get the kind of education that you think he should get, you can consider it an opportunity. Appropriate education to meet his needs is a judgment call. You know your child better than anyone else, and you know what would be best.

The important thing is to be courageous to request what your child needs. If what you request is not available, or if teachers need more training in certain areas, you may have to find ways to make it happen. Many school districts have special funds for teacher training or special equipment. There are also many service clubs, such as Rotary, Lions, Kiwanis, or Soroptomists, that provide donations for specific needs in the community. I know one boy with cerebral palsy who was able to receive a specialized computer from one of these community service organizations so that he could do his homework assignments at home. Another little girl received a piece of mobility equipment from a special fund in the school district to help her increase her ability to stand and walk. Sisters that have a genetic disorder were able to get funds to send their teacher to a conference on their particular disease. Other sources of funding may be local churches, national organizations such as United Cerebral Palsy, or local or national corporations that may be looking for a good tax write-off.

In conclusion, do not feel that you must sacrifice your desires or your child's needs. Do not just quietly accept whatever the educational system has to offer. If you feel your rights have been violated, discuss the problem with the teacher and/or the principal first. If you cannot seem to get results, you may need to take the matter up through the educational system. If that fails you may opt for "due process" or "mediation," a legal means by which important decisions or compromises may be made on behalf of your child. To better understand your rights and the legal provisions for due process, you may contact your State Department of Education, Special Education Division. They should be able to clarify regulations and send you information on how to go about appealing any decisions made by the I.E.P. team. Like in the field of medical care, there are numerous organizations that exist for the sole purpose of helping parents through the I.E.P. process to get what the children need. Usually, they are listed right in the Yellow Pages, or ask a social worker to help you locate one. If you need more information on resources available to you, *Exceptional Parent Magazine* puts out an annual resource guide that is very comprehensive. Please see the appendix on catalogs and books for the address and phone number. Keep fighting for what you know your child needs, and remain closely involved in his or her education. Nothing will benefit you more than having an ongoing positive working relationship with those who can provide what your little one needs. There are so many incredible teachers and programs out there! You can access them if you are persistent!

Advocacy in Services Provided

When I was going through particularly hard times and had injured my shoulder as a result of lifting Dana so much, I decided it was time to get more help in our home. My husband and I had to go through a tremendously draining process of fighting for what we needed at a time when I felt at my weakest. We appealed the decisions made by agencies in our area about how much in-home support they would provide for us. This meant going through the process of an "informal hearing" to voice our grievances to the hearing officer and hope that she would see things our way. She didn't. That sent us on the journey to the next step of appeal, which is a formal state hearing in the presence of a judge. I had been convinced by some well-meaning friends that this was too large a project to take on without some legal help, so we hired a lawyer for a thankfully nominal fee. I'm not sure that was the wisest decision for our particular case. Bringing in a lawyer made us into the aggressors and put the agencies on the defense. Even the judge had a very poor opinion of us after the whole ordeal was over. However, with the help of our legal counsel who knew the laws of our state, we were able to secure a full-time personal attendant to care for our daughter for a year. My shoulder had a chance to heal, and so did my mental well being. Was it worth the hassle and stress? I will offer a tentative "yes."

In another instance, I once again decided to appeal the decisions regarding the services that would be offered to my daughter. This time I decided to take my own advice. I went into the informal hearing well prepared. I had typed up an outline of exactly what I wished to discuss. Firstly, I requested that the agency personnel define the purpose for the existence of the agency. It came out that the agency's reason for being was for the purpose of assisting families to stay together and to be able to care for their children in the home environment for as long as possible. Basically, they were there to save the state a lot of money because it costs a lot less to help a family to care for its own than to run a state institution. So then, I outlined my understanding of what they were willing to offer to Dana. I followed with the history that had led up to my complaint. I stated the reasons why my requests filled the ultimate goals of the agency and how they met the criteria for the agency's provision using their own definition given earlier. In other words, I was able to clearly give a reason why the services I was requesting would help keep our family together and Dana out of an institution. I then clearly stated my request once again and opened the table for questions and discussion. It was at that time that I was so glad I had brought Dana's teacher with me to the meeting. She was a neutral party who happened to be an expert in the knowledge of Dana's needs. Her input was extremely valuable to my arguments. By the end of the hearing, the hearing officer, instead of being hostile and defensive, saw me as a rational human being and actually joined my side of the argument! She even asked for a copy of my outline so that she could take it to her superiors! Dana was eventually able to receive a service that I considered essential for her care and happiness. Granted, I was not asking for as much as when I pulled in the lawyer, and I did win the case in both instances, but this second appeal was so much easier. I did not have to go to a state hearing before a judge. I felt that I was in control of the meeting and my own reputation. Even better, the agency and I started to work together, instead of against each other. They seem to respect me now, and I believe that they would do even more for Dana if I were to request it. There was little stress. There were few bad feelings. Most importantly, my daughter has benefited greatly. The bottom line is, you must come prepared and professional. Show why your requests fit the objectives of the agency. Do what you have to do, but try to fight with a smile.

If you would like help or further information, call Disabilities Rights Education/Defense at (510) 644-2555. They are located at 2212 Sixth Street in Berkeley, California 94710. This is a service organization that serves nationwide for information, technical assistance and training, and referral services for people with disabilities and parents of children with disabilities. They specialize in disability civil rights laws and the Americans with Disabilities Act.

Another source of help may be the National Information Center for Children and Youth with Disabilities. Their address is P.O. Box 1492, Washington, D.C. 20013. They may be reached at (800) 695-0285 or (202) 884-8200. There, you will find someone who can answer specific questions, give referrals to sources of help, organizations, and publications. These services are free. Be sure to take advantage of them.

I now live in another state. I find that everything is different. Now I am not just trying to get more services for my daughter; I am trying to get services period. There was not enough funding in the state's budget for services to the disabled last year, and now there is a waiting list of people who have been denied services altogether until there is further funding! I find myself in the middle of a lobbying campaign at the state level to get the needed funding to provide the services needed to care for persons with disabilities. This is a situation I never dreamed I would ever encounter in the United States. Third world countries, yes, but not here. Everyday is a new adventure as I make phone calls and write letters to my legislators to gently lead them to an understanding of the gravity of this situation and how it effects our family specifically. The good news is that this is a great country. God bless democracy! We individual parents do have a voice. You and I can make a difference for our own children and for others who benefit from the changes we instigate!

One last note about advocacy: **be careful of becoming over-zealous — for your sake and for the sake of your child.**

Firstly, if it seems like you are always in fighting mode with all service providers and school officials, they will take notice. You run the risk of being labeled a troublemaker, and you will not be taken seriously. I know that a red flag goes up in my mind every time I meet a parent who seems to take pride in being an adversary to all service providers. You are an advocate, not an adversary.

Secondly, your first responsibility remains with your child and your family. Be very careful to keep things in balance. You can easily become so involved in advocating for services that you neglect the ones who count most. You can become unavailable to your family at times when they need you most. Good communication can cease, and you may find yourself with a lot more problems that just school non-compliance.

Thirdly, the little one you are fighting for, more than anything in the world, needs to feel your love. If you are too wrapped up in meetings and litigation, you may not be giving him what he needs most. You may find that you are always agitated or upset because of having to fight your causes. This doesn't help. Remember what I said at the outset of this book, that the best thing you can give to your child is a mother (or father) who is content. Just be very mindful to weigh everything in a balance before choosing your battles.

The Dream Keeper
— Langston Hughes

Bring me all of your dreams,
You dreamers,
Bring me all of your
Heart melodies
That I may wrap them
In a blue cloud-cloth
Away from the too-rough fingers
Of the world.

7

Planning
Your Estate Carefully

When God closes a door, He opens a window.
— Unknown

I know of some people who had a son late in life who had developmental delays. They had worked very hard and long to give him the very best opportunities in life that could help mold him into a contributing citizen of the community. He had been "mainstreamed" into a regular middle school and high school, and had played on a special baseball team for four years. When he turned adult, he was set up in a nice little apartment that he shared with a roommate. He worked a part-time job at a fast food restaurant just down the street from his apartment. These parents were also able to get him on Social Security supports to help him with his living expenses that weren't covered by the income he made from his job. When their son was twenty-eight years old, the mother died of a heart attack. A year later, the father contracted cancer and did not last long. During his last few days, this father, wanting to make sure that everything would be in order for his son with special needs, made out his final will. He left everything in his son's name so that the son would never have to worry about money. Everything was taken care of, right? Wrong.

There are important financial considerations that could greatly effect your child's financial support in the future. Do you know that your little one will not be able to receive Social Security benefits when she becomes an adult if it could be shown that she owns more than $2000.00 in her name? This being the case, think about the story above. After Uncle Sam claimed inheritance taxes, the young man in the story was left with a modest bank account and no governmental supports. He did not earn enough from his job at the restaurant to even pay his rent. Eventually, his needs ate away at the funds in the bank until he was left with nothing but his meager wages. Only then could he get back on governmental support, and then it was not enough for him to keep his apartment. He had to go and live in a group home. The home was too far away from his place of employment for him to walk, and there was no bus route nearby, so he quit. He ended up just watching the television all day letting others take care of him. Everything that his parents had worked for was gone.

This tale may seem a bit extreme, but it represents what is true for many Americans. How then can we parents possibly set aside enough money to cover the entire cost of our children's care if we were to die? Their Social Security could be cut off if they inherit anything. On the other hand, Social Security benefits alone would leave our children in severe poverty. The reality is that they will need both the social financial support and any other income available from an estate or a job in order to cover the cost of their care and living expenses. If we were all multi-millionaires, we wouldn't need to worry so much, but there is little chance we regular folk can possibly save up enough to cover the cost of help and care for our children without some government help stepping in.

My husband and I went to a professional estate planner who was well versed in laws about persons with disabilities. We found that for our own circumstances, it was best to set up a Living Trust and a Special Needs Trust to ensure that Dana's financial needs would be taken care of. A Living Trust is a legal entity in and of itself and so becomes the "owner" of all you have. You can put your house in its name, your bank accounts, your stocks, your 401(K) plan, etc. Everything you own, you own in the name of the Trust. You can have complete control over all of your assets just as if they were all in your names, but because everything is in the name of a trust, when you die you essentially have no estate to leave behind. Everything is owned by the trust and continues to be owned by the trust. There is no estate, so there is no hefty inheritance tax that needs to be paid. All of the monies and assets are still available to your heirs, but they are saved from having to pay the burdensome tax. In addition, you may then specify in your trust that at your death, a portion (that you determine ahead of time) should go into a Special Needs Trust that has been set up for the care of your child with special needs. Therefore, the

Special Needs Trust then becomes the legal owner of the funds that are available for your child's care, including any investments, savings, real estate, life insurance policies, etc. Because the trust is the owner of the assets, your child still does not own anything in his name, and is able to receive benefits from the trust as well as the Social Security Benefits due him. Also, the money is immediately available for his care instead of being held up in a complicated probate. You will have named in the Special Needs Trust the names of the persons that you wish to have as trustees (those who take care of the financial matters for your child after you are gone). In a perfect world, this person, or people, would be the financially responsible sort who care about your little one and will be sure to work closely with the person you have named in your will as guardian of your child.

In all honesty, I do not have an overabundance of assets and investments; not many of us do. I do not have a big estate to worry about in the first place. I hardly have enough to pay the lawyer, much less enough to set aside for Dana's care. For that reason, my husband and I began by setting up a life insurance policy with the Special Needs Trust as the actual beneficiary. We pay a reasonably sized premium once a year to insure that the trust account has enough value to help take care of Dana. We have since added a savings account to the trust as well. It is very important that you let everyone in your family know that if they wish to leave some inheritance for your child, it should be left in the name of the Special Needs Trust! You wouldn't want a simple thing like the inheritance of three thousand dollars from Great-grandpa George to hinder your child's ability to collect benefits. It can go into this special savings account and everybody is happy. I cannot express what a great peace of mind it gives to know that our little loved one will be well attended to after we are gone.

It may seem to you like this is going a bit too far. "After all," you may say, "I am still young. What is the likelihood that something is going to happen to me?" True. Not a lot of young people think about such things as estate planning. Let me suggest, though, that you have a responsibility above and beyond the normal person. You have been given a special charge that requires special considerations. You need to act responsibly on behalf of your child both for now and for the future. His well-being could be at stake.

Each state has different laws about estate planning for persons with disabilities. Most are difficult to navigate. You may want to contact your state Bar Association. They may be able to tell you if there are any lawyers specializing in estate planning for the disabled. I have found them to be very helpful and courteous, and they will be able to connect you with a specialist in your area. If not, publications for people with disabilities and their families, often advertise companies who provide estate planning services.

At the very least, if you have not already done so, sit down and write up a very clear will. Do it today. There are even do-it-yourself forms for writing your own will that can be found at most stationery stores. There are also programs for your computer. Include preferences for whom you wish to care for your child, as well as second choices in case your first choice of a guardian would not be available. Name an executor as the person you want to be in charge of handling the will and the distribution of the estate. List any other special instructions or preferences very concisely. Lastly, have the will signed by a notary public. That would at least be a start.

With the will, you should include what is called a Letter of Intent. This is an idea that was first made well known by L. Mark Russell in his book, *Planning for the Future*. It is this letter that you can use to pass along any useful information to whomever will be your child's care-giver. They will need to know the child's family history, medical history, doctor's names, daily routine, likes and dislikes, favorite foods, favorite activities, hygienic needs, toileting habits, religious preference, important social service organizations, case manager's names, special equipment, family traditions, and special requests. Obviously, you will want to update this information from time to time, because much of the information will change as your child grows. I keep mine on a disk so that I can pop it into a computer and make changes quickly and easily. You need not notarize the Letter of Intent and it may be in your own handwriting. Just be sure to keep it with all of the other important papers regarding your estate. Keep them in a safe place, and make sure that others know where to find them.

This has been a very brief run-down of a few things you may want to think about. I recommend Mark Russell's book as an excellent resource that can take you much further into the subject of providing for your special child's future. Russell wrote it specifically to parents of children with disabilities. He discusses the role of government benefits in your child's life and takes the mystery out of guardianship. He provides many good examples of his topics and provides a thorough model of a Letter of Intent. The book has become a highly recommended volume. It is a little bit intimidating, though. It is a rather thick book, which has been out since the early nineties. However, if you can manage to read it through, you will have most of your questions answered and can steer into the future with a lot more confidence.

Why?

— Author unknown

On the street I saw a small girl
Cold and shivering in a thin dress,
With little hope of a decent meal.
I became angry and said to
God:
"Why did you permit this?
Why don't you do something
About it?"
For awhile God said nothing.
That night he replied, quite suddenly:
"I certainly did something about it.
I made you."

8

Considering
Placement And Other Options

Be strong and of good courage. Do not be dismayed.
— Joshua 1:9

Becky and John are just eighteen years old. They had started dating during their senior year in high school. A couple of weeks after graduation, Becky discovered she was pregnant. Getting married seemed to be the responsible thing to do, even though Becky was still living at home with her parents and had not yet found a job. John was still working his summer job at the tire store before going off to college in another town to study business. Of course, marriage would change those plans, but there was a child to think about now. So, two months later, they were exchanging vows at the altar, promising rich lives of love and joy to each other.

John had been able to keep his job at the tire store, but the hours were long, the job paid little, and he was tired. Becky was terribly sick during the next few months. Almost all of the household responsibilities fell on John. The only thing that seemed to get him though the day was thinking about playing ball with his little son some sunny afternoon in the distant future. That dream was beginning to take the place of his dreams for a degree in business. Becky could only think of holding that dear, sweet little baby in her arms and rocking it to sleep every night.

The doctor finally had to put Becky on bed rest, and despite the efforts to subdue premature contractions, the baby was born a lot earlier than expected. Now John and Becky are sitting in a little consultation room at the hospital, overwhelmed and frightened. The doctor explains to the young couple that the child has abnormal brain development, with very little cortex and signs of hydrocephalus. In his opinion there is very little hope that this child will ever develop beyond the functioning level of a three-month-old infant. At the end of the consultation with the physician, Becky and John are encouraged to place the child directly into institutional care and to not take him home. They sit silent and stunned. Is this a dream? What are the implications? What if they decide to take their new son home? What would life be like? Can they even stand to think of living their lives having to take care of a — a brain damaged child?

Alice's husband, Bob, recently died suddenly from a bacterial infection. There were few signs he was even sick until it was too late. She shares how he had always been so healthy. She was always sure that she would be the first to go, and even then in old age. Bob's death is made even more tragic by their family circumstances. He was a big man and was always the one who could manage to handle their only son, Matt, when he lashed out in uncontrollable fits of anger caused by his disability. Alice is just a petite woman. She knows that she will not be able to manage Matt all by herself. He is built like his father, and she fears she is in danger of being physically hurt by Matt, now that he is such a sturdy young man. She knows that she needs the help that her husband can no longer give.

The subject of placement is very touchy. Everyone's experiences are different. The extra demands brought about by a child's disabilities are many and varied. Some parents seem to be put together in a way that can easily accept and handle the challenges. Others are not. The actual decision of whether or not to place a child out of the home is so subjective and individual that there are really no concrete guidelines to offer. I can say that the policy of any assisting governmental agencies these days is typically to maintain the child in the home environment for as long as possible. The main purpose for the existence of most of these agencies is to train, support, and enable persons and families to live functionally with disabilities. However, they recognize that there are instances when a child can become violent and so disruptive as to threaten the well-being of other family members. Also, parents may believe it best to find out-of-home placement when the child reaches the age when normal children would naturally be leaving the home. Perhaps this could also be in the best interest of the adult child. In this section I will try to discuss some of the different options available.

We have all heard horror stories about institutions for children and adults with special needs. There are stories of abuse, mistreatment, neglect, illegal medical practices, etc. These are atrocities that none of us would wish our children to experience. Unfortunately, some of these practices do still exist.

I was struck by a report I heard recently about a new technique for developing communication among autistic patients. The results of using this new technique were truly astounding, but the stories behind the lives of the people benefiting from a new-found communication were what touched me deeply. Some of the residents of a facility for severely disabled adults had been receiving behavioral modification treatments that included shock therapy among other forms of discipline. This was all done in the name of "training" in order to decrease undesirable behaviors such as screaming or self-destructive behaviors such as biting oneself. What was remarkable was that when these individuals had finally found a way to express themselves, many of them remarked that they wanted the treatments to stop. They fully understood that their actions were undesirable, but they were simply unable to control themselves, no mater how often they were shocked. Imagine a life like that! Actually, what was even more astounding was that these people found it in their hearts to forgive those who had been training them. I cannot conceive how the parents must have felt upon finding out for the first time how their children had suffered under a facility's chosen form of discipline.

I admit that even parents don't always know what is best for their children at all times, especially if the child cannot communicate. However, the information gained from these autistic individuals underscores the importance that the parents carefully screen facilities and be continually and actively involved in any sort of placement. We cannot allow mistreatment, even under the best intentions, to continue. The good news is that there are so many really wonderful options now available. Resources can range from full residential nursing care facilities to day programs. There are group homes. There is short-term respite care so that the rest of your family may be able to take a vacation. Some organizations offer summer camps, and others specialize in children with challenging behavioral problems. There is a directory of facilities across the United States that can be found in better libraries called *The Directory For Exceptional Children.* It can provide good information about various placements and programs, but gives no recommendations. Some states have Regional Centers, others have a Department of Human Services. Either should be able to provide you with information about local accommodations and programs. Your state agency or social worker should know of other sources of information.

According to the "alternative residential model," there are four levels of service for residential facilities. Level One provides basic board and care with general supervision, but offers no scheduled activities or training. This would be appropriate for very capable individuals. Level Two is a homelike setting, giving training in activities of daily living and a moderate amount of supervision for persons with basic self-care skills. A Level Three facility is also homelike. It offers a more structured environment. There is training and instruction to enable residents to participate more fully in the basic activities of self-care and daily living. Those residents whose behavioral or physical challenges are so great that their needs cannot be met in other facilities would gain the most from the highly structured Level Four facility.

Please note that the majority of these residential care facilities are community group homes. They are often owner-operated foster homes. You may also wish to search for Medicaid homes, which come highly recommended because of the medical staff they provide. In any case, you must do thorough research. You should request a specific description of instructional methods and techniques, including methodology for measuring training outcomes. You also need to know staff qualifications, duties, and hours. Ask about licensing and assessment for the facility. How does it measure its effectiveness? Demand references, and if anything seems to be the slightest bit suspicious, such as requiring girls only, check it out very carefully or look for other options. Make sure that the placement location has a 24-hour open door policy, so that you may visit at any time. You may even choose to do personal background checks of the staff through public records. Do not assume that the hiring agency completed these background checks. I had a person helping me with my daughter in my home that had come through a reputable local medical care agency. This individual later admitted to having been convicted of child molestation five years prior. I got sick just thinking that I had entrusted my daughter into the care of this person, assuming that the agency had done its homework.

Again, most people and agencies believe that in-home placement is best for the family. There are many laws recently passed to help parents get the help and support they need to keep children at home. It makes sense. It costs the government about one third the cost of residential care to provide support services in the home, and the lawmakers are finally becoming aware of this. Unfortunately, it usually takes a lawyer to point out these new laws to the government agencies providing the services. If you would like to have help with the care of your child in your home, you are entitled to respite care services through your Regional Center or through other agencies, such as Social Security or the Human Services Department in your state. There are federal waiver laws that passed not long ago that provide for federal funding of equipment or personal attendant care in the home. The waiver means that your child can qualify for federal and state support on the basis of their needs and income, alone. Get to know these laws. It is possible that if the family shows sufficient need, such as physical or emotional inability to care for the child, one can receive full-time care in the home. However, if you wish to receive more than twelve hours of help per month, you may need to prepare yourself for a fight.

As if it is not enough that we have to face the day to day adversities of being parents of special children, we have to expend an enormous amount of energy just to get services that are rightfully ours. After all, this is what we pay taxes for. Different regions of the U.S. vary greatly in what they can provide, and it helps to know the laws of your state regarding persons with disabilities. Unfortunately, you may have to do this research yourself, or you may wish to seek legal council. The best source of advice still seems to be word of mouth. Contact with other parents can provide priceless information, so make it a point to be involved with other special parents. You can also get copies of your state's laws by calling the State Department of Human Services (it may go under a different name in your state) and ask. You will probably be transferred to a chain of people who can't answer your questions, but eventually, you will get to someone who knows how you can get the information you need. Hang in there, and be patient.

Other options that are available are international au pair or nanny organizations. Many young people would like to come to the U.S. for a year of adventure and to learn English. There are agencies throughout Europe that find American employment for young people of their country who are seeking it. A great place to search is on the internet. Even the Yellow Pages list nanny placement agencies if you are interested in a local agency. Just be aware that this can be a very costly option.

For those of us on more modest budgets, there are many students here in the U.S. that would do just about anything for free room and board. They usually have flexible schedules. They are young and strong enough to do lifting. Most are searching for new ways to bring in an extra little bit of income. The best situation is if you have a college or university near your home that offers majors in medicine, physical or occupational therapy, special education, child development, nursing, or social services. Although any student could be a great help, students from any of these curriculums could get a lot out of the hands-on experience of working and living within a family that has special needs. You may want to place an advertisement with the housing department of the college or with the dean of a particular school. Just be sure to write up a clear contract as to what the job responsibilities would be and what compensation will be offered. Don't forget to include a clause that gets them out of your house if things don't work out! Don't let that possibility scare you off, however. This type of help has been very successful for most people who have tried it.

If adoption seems to be the necessary course, and let me tenderly admit that it may be in some circumstances, it may be very helpful to contact the National Adoption Center at (800) 862-3678, or write to them at 1500 Walnut street, Suite 701, Philadelphia, PA 19102. They are known for promoting adoption opportunities throughout the United States, especially for children with special needs. Please be sure to consider all options.

To All Parents
— Edgar A. Guest

"I'll lend you for a little time
a child of mine," He said,
"For you to love the while she lives
and mourn for when she's dead.
It may be six or seven years
or twenty-two or three,
But will you, till I call her back
take care of her for Me?
She'll bring her charms to gladden you
and should her stay be brief,
You'll have her lovely memories
as solace for your grief.

"I cannot promise she will stay,
since all from earth return,
But there are lessons taught down there
I want this child to learn.
I've looked the wide world over,
in my search for teachers true
And from the throngs that crowd life's lanes,
I have selected you.
Now will you give her all your love,
nor think the labor vain,

Nor hate Me when I come to call
*   to take her back again?"*

I fancied that I hear them say:
*   "Dear Lord, Thy will be done!*
For all the joy Thy child shall bring,
*   the risk of grief we'll run.*
We'll shelter her with tenderness,
*   we'll love her while we may,*
And for the happiness we've known
*   forever grateful stay;*
But shall the angels call for her
*   much sooner than we'd planned,*
We'll brave the bitter grief that comes
*   and try to understand."*

9

HAVING A HEART-TO-HEART

Tough times never last, but tough people do.
— Robert H. Schuller

Inarguably, the most valuable thing anyone has ever done for me is to give me the permission to allow myself to admit my true emotions. To grieve when I needed to grieve. To be down when I felt like being down. To go ahead and be full of joy when I really felt full of joy. To be real. To forgive myself. To give myself permission not to try to be something I am not. Above all else, this is how I have survived and been able to play out the hand that life dealt me. When it came to discovering that my daughter was born with severe disabilities and that I was going to be a "special parent," I found it hard to know what emotions to feel and how to express them. My mother-in-law once put her hand on my knee and said, "It's O.K. to cry, Honey." I tried, but I couldn't. I was numb and confused. However, at least I was able to accept that those were normal and real reactions. Other parents may respond to the same situation differently, and that is O.K., too. After all, how is one supposed to act when you've been dealt a blow? You may cry, you may quiet down, you may scream, you may punch the wall. You may need a hug. You may push all others away. Allow yourself permission to be true to your gut emotions.

THE VALLEY

Even those of us parents who seem like we "have it all together" go through times of insanity. It happened to me, too. When Dana was six, I found myself in the darkest time of my life. Worse still, I saw no way out. The emotions I was feeling had been the most negative I could remember. I was afraid that my depression was affecting my ability to function. It was also affecting all of my most dearly loved ones around me. I had a great turbulence inside. I feared I was going to lose my self-control and possibly my self. I was experiencing memory lapses and disorganization (even more than usual!). I was unable to keep up with daily chores. Apathy was my closest friend. I was shutting down, and I was sure that it was all related to my struggles and frustrations with Dana's disabilities.

You see, I was told by some careless person very early on to expect that Dana would reach her maximum potential by age seven or eight. The neurologist who was seeing my daughter reassured me that this was not true. He said that the brain continues to develop into adulthood. I should expect to see her continuing to increase in her abilities and learning well beyond her young childhood. That answer appeased me for quite a while until that fated age of seven approached.

Following is an excerpt from my journal:

This last year has been a year of looking back and reassessing Dana's progress. Some of the conclusions I have made are that:

- *She is six years old and still doesn't seem to like to do much other than suck on her fingers.*
- *I still have to go down the infant isle in the toy store to find her anything to play with.*
- *Physical therapy has made no progress in two years and is strictly maintenance at this point.*
- *Occupational therapy at 7:30 in the morning twenty miles away is a pain in the neck, and her therapist has admitted that she doesn't think that Dana will ever be feeding herself; although, that's what she is still working on!*

I'm having a hard time getting over the hump into acceptance; I am realizing that maybe I am upset about this because I really don't accept Dana fully for what she is and who she is right now. I want more.

There was an argument going on inside of me. I kept asking myself, "What else can we try in order to help her increase her abilities?" Maybe we haven't done everything we can for her. On the other hand, there was also a very present sense of "Why bother? Is it really worth the effort?" I kept wondering if I needed to simply do what I could to make sure Dana was comfortable and happy, and leave it at that. Or should I keep working on trying to make her "do more?" Should I be the miracle Mom who works for ten long years so that her daughter can grasp a peg for five seconds? We'd been considering setting up a computer terminal for her here at home. It would be just one more thing for her to do. However, was it really worth pushing? Would she ever be able to use the computer in a way that would really enhance her life? Up until that time, she had used it with a great deal of assistance in order to make the computer sing a song. Big deal. But, then again, did she enjoy it? Would the computer make her life happier and richer? Probably. It's certainly better than sitting and sucking on one's fingers. Let's face it, most children begin to learn computer skills with simple games, right? She was only six. But, was it worth spending the money to buy a power pad and set up a workstation for her here at home? And would I put the time in that's necessary to help her work on it? I was already frustrated that I couldn't get my work done. It was taking all of my energy just to do the most basic housework. When would I get the laundry done? I asked myself over and over, "How do others do it!"

These feelings, of course, just added to the guilt. To make matters even worse, Dana was not sleeping well. I was covering the "night duty" so that my husband could get sleep enough to function the next day at work. "Clinical depression and sleep deprivation" was what one person called it. All I know is that I would wake up in the middle of the night and cry until my pillow was wet. I would sit on the shower floor and yell at God in anger! I remember in particular one perfectly beautiful Sunday morning. The entire family had gone to church, myself included. There was nothing exceptional about the day until, upon arriving home with my girls in tow, I simply sat down on the couch and wept out loud for about an hour. My three-year-old just stood in the hallway and watched with curiosity.

One night when I was especially exhausted, I heard Dana crying again and imagined that she was laughing at me. Everything inside of me was longing to get up out of bed, go to her room, and hold a pillow over her face until she stopped breathing. Thus, I would be putting both of us out of our misery. I began to sob terribly with guilt. How could I ever think I was a good mother if I could allow myself to contemplate killing my child? "I must be the most terrible person in the world," I told myself.

I wonder how many stories I have heard are similar — stories of little Billy "drowning" in the bathtub, or of little Missy who "just didn't wake up in the morning." I sadly acknowledge that these tragedies do happen, but how many of these are actually cases where parents could no longer cope with the extraordinary demands placed on them by a child with special needs? Even parents who do not have those extra demands can go over the edge. We hear it on the news all of the time. We hear of a mother who locks her babies in a car and drives it into the river. We hear of babies being found in trash bins. Studies on sudden infant death syndrome (SIDS) reveal that of the babies who were thought to have died from SIDS, a few may have actually died at their parents' hands. It is quite obvious that these feelings of frustration and inability to cope are very common and natural. In fact, I would go so far as to say that almost every parent feels a tinge of despair at some time. *It is so crucial that we recognize this as natural, so that we as the parents can go to a friend or to a professional (or even to a journal) and seek a way to express these feelings that will not be detrimental to others or to ourselves.*

You may be feeling inadequate, guilty, angry, frustrated, confused, hurt, numb, frazzled, exhausted, abandoned, or frightened. You may even be feeling encouraged, strong, and ready to tackle the world. All are valid feelings. In my own case, I was able to work out those negative feelings eventually. I sought out help on many levels. My family was supportive, and I asked friends to be patient. Someone I greatly respect reminded me that I am normal, after all. I also approached my state services and requested more help with Dana's day-to-day care, so that I would be relieved for a while, until I felt I could tackle the world again. I even took a dream vacation of camping by myself in the mountains for a few days. It took time, but it happened. I will lead no one to believe that I don't have some struggles now, but through time, experience and a little effort, I have learned to accept them and deal with them in a more constructive way. The bottom line is that my daughter has a mother who is now sound and happy. I am ready and able to take care of her needs, physical and emotional, and thus build for both of us a more fulfilling and happy life. That is true wealth.

If you find yourself identifying with these experiences, you are not alone. Nor are you a bad person. You are completely normal. Please allow yourself forgiveness. Seek out an understanding person with whom you can share and ask them to help you. There is an abundance of professionals out there who are trained in grief counseling and depression management. Medical insurance is even beginning to cover the expenses for this kind of help. Friends are great sources of support and can be very helpful if they are able to just listen and not judge. Clergy are also likely to be able to help you through tough feelings and frustrations. In my case, I was so embarrassed and guilty about my feelings, I wasn't sure I could share them with anyone else, so I chose to open up to myself by means of a journal. That allowed me to confront my thoughts and look at myself face to face.

It may be particularly difficult to open up to your spouse for many reasons. We are usually taught to be strong and supportive of our spouses. It may be difficult to ask for them to be supportive of us. Deep inside there may be the fear that if we show ourselves to be weak our spouse will no longer love us. Sometimes, our spouse is a little too close to the problems and feelings at hand. In that case, it is best to seek a professional. That is what they are there for. It is so unfortunate that there is a certain stigma attached to seeking professional advice. Don't let that keep you from getting the help that may be essential to your mental health and your relationships with loved ones. Don't be afraid to take full advantage of all of the help that is out there for you. It will be the best thing you could ever do for yourself and your child, because he or she depends on you, your strength and your love.

THE MOUNTAIN TOPS

In contrast, let me tell of another side of life. I've mentioned in previous chapters that I have to look for and focus on the little joys that can be found in life with a daughter with severe challenges. For example, I love the evenings when it is time to wash the dishes. Don't get me wrong. I hate washing dishes, but I love the joy that permeates our house during that dreaded chore. Dana is the perpetrator. She can't see much at all and has great difficulty controlling her body, but she can hear. Different sounds are her greatest pleasure in life. Dishes clattering are definitely on the "top ten" list. How can you help but find joy in life when you hear squeals of glee coming from behind you every time you drop a plate into the sink. The whole house seems to join in the uproarious laughter when I drop a pan lid on the floor and say, "Uh-oh!" Dana goes into uncontrollable rounds of belly-deep chuckles at that sound. So, I often just drop one on purpose.

I will never forget when Dana learned to make a "snort" sound with her nose. I was lying in bed with her at about 12:30 a.m., trying to get her to calm down enough to go back to sleep. As I was talking to her, in the midst of her sobs and much to her surprise she came out with a great big snort. Her eyes lit up and a smile spread across her face as if she had just discovered the winning ticket of the lottery! With enormous effort, she managed to get herself to do it again. I laughed and snorted back at her. So it went well into the early hours of the morning; a joyful chorus of snorts and laughter. I thought to myself, "This is great!"

I would not be satisfied with just a snort at face value, however. I just had to find some way to make more of this new-found skill my daughter had landed upon. I was pretty sure that Channel 7 wouldn't be very aggressive at putting it on the six o'clock news. I got a few "hmphhh"s from family members, but that didn't satisfy me. Then, I remembered the petting zoo that was in a nearby town. Oh, this was too good to be true! I just had to take her there so we could snort with the pigs! Sure enough, there were two little potbellied piglets waiting for us. We were able to pick them up and stick them in Dana's face while both parties snorted at each other. This has been an indelible picture in my mind ever since.

Another indelible picture I have hangs on the wall in my hallway. It is a simple family portrait—in fact, you'll find it on page 135. I do not necessarily get nostalgic and think of what a precious family I have whenever I see the portrait. I often just remember what a time we had with the photographer that day. Let's face it. We'll do anything to get our kids to smile for a portrait. Just the thought brings images of gentlemen with squeaky little yellow ducks and teddy bears dancing in the air beside a camera. It only follows then that since Dana likes strange sounds so much we should take full advantage of sounds that make her laugh. You haven't lived until you've sat in a photo studio listening to the photographer imitate the sounds of all sorts of unacceptable and embarrassing bodily functions! We laughed until our sides hurt. That portrait will probably always be one of my favorites.

Lastly, I will always cherish the image of Dana on a hot afternoon in May, sitting in her wheelchair in the middle of a horse rink. I got this one on videotape. She had just ridden in her first horse show after a year of equestrian physical therapy. She sat there with an assistant who was helping her to clutch a large trophy topped with a golden horse. The grin on her face was indescribable. It was the first time I had ever seen her just glowing with pride! Maybe her sister could give dance recitals and read all by herself, but this was Dana's turn. This was Dana's triumph. She could ride a horse!

I cried, of course.

Why am I relating all of these stories? These are the moments that can make the difference. These are the moments that will help me to get through the tough times with some element of balance in my life. To use the image of the poker hand, these are my "aces in the hole." What has your child done to make you laugh? Surely, there is something. Mark the day on your calendar in red. Create for yourself a mental image and file it in a safe place in your mind. Pull it out and refer to it when you need a lift. Constantly be on the lookout for little moments to add to your mental file. Exercise those memories often, but live for the little joys of today. Remember that any cards, even deuces and threes, can make up a winning hand!

By the way, I never did set up the computer room for Dana. She likes to swing in the back yard instead.

My Recipe For Lemonade

There is an old saying, "If life gives you lemons, make lemonade!" Lately, that is just what I have been doing, for living with a disabled child is a process of learning to cope with and make the most of every given day. This is my recipe for keeping a smile on my face and a spring in my step.

First, you must prepare your work surface. Realize that you can't turn back the clock. So take what you've been given and ask yourself, "What am I going to do about it?"

Begin with three full measures of communication with your spouse. Talking openly about our daughter Dana, her problems, and our feelings about the situation has allowed us to reach a point of acceptance which I think is critical to coping.

Blend this with one bunch of doing something. I have found that keeping busy with a purpose has done more for my self-esteem and for my relationship with my daughter than anything else. I am constantly looking for new ways to teach and interact with her. It gives my life meaning and direction.

Next, sift through your schedule to keep a balance in your life. If you are like most special parents, you have an incredible schedule of doctor's visits, therapy, infant stimulation, physical therapy exercises, etc. These are all wonderful, but I feel it is also important to garnish this with a trip to the park to smell the flowers or with cuddling in a rocking chair while reading a book. After all, Dana is a child first, and a child with handicaps second.

While sifting, be sure to take some time out for yourself and your marriage, too. There is an amazing amount of stress in just the day-to-day routine activities with a disabled child. For this reason, my husband and I make extra sure that we get out about once a week (even for a burger). The baby-sitter doesn't cost that much, and our marriage and sanity are priceless.

While you are mixing all of this together, a lot of emotions can get stirred up. I have bad days, too, but I allow myself to have them. Why fight them? Just get it out and get it over with.

Be careful not to whip up the future too much. None of us knows if we'll even be here tomorrow, so why waste time trying to imagine what it might be like? Instead, work on making it the best possible. Someone once said, "Pray like everything depends on God, and work like everything depends on you."

As my recipe has become more seasoned, I have found that, although I would have it different, it's okay that Dana is the way she is. She may not be like every other child, but she is a person in her own right and very beautiful in her own way. Not much has helped me cope with her differences more than loving her for who she is and applauding all of the little triumphs in her life.

Appendix

RESOURCES

CATOLOGUES, MAGAZINES AND DIRECTORIES

Enabling Devices and Toys for Special Children, Inc.
385 Warburton Avenue
Hastings-On-Hudson, New York 10706
(914) 478-0960
www.enablingdevices.com
A wonderful collection of brightly-colored, interesting toys, as well as ingenious alternative communication devices.

Enrichments
P.O. Box 471
Western Springs, IL 60558-0471
A catalog of products for enhancing abilities and the quality of life for persons with physical challenges.

Kaplan Concepts for Exceptional Children
P.O. Box 609
Lewisville, NC 27023-0609
(800)-334-2014
www.kaplanco.com
This catalog is full of educational items for children with special needs including toys, equipment, books and music.

Sammons Preston
P.O. Box 5071
Bolingbrook, IL 60440
(800)-323-5547
www.sammonspreston.com
An excellent source for health care and rehabilitation products.

Special Populations by Flaghouse, Inc.
150 North MacQuesten Parkway
Mount Vernon, New York 10550
(800)-793-7900
www.flaghouse.com
This is one of the best sources of a great variety of products for the disabled. Teachers and therapists use this to order their equipment, adaptive devices, and playthings.

Exceptional Parent Magazine
P.O. Box 3000, Dept EP
Denville, NJ 07834
(800) 247-8080
www.eparent.com
Through this magazine you may discover things available for your child that you never dreamed existed. A great source of relief and support. This magazine also puts out an extensive resource catalog once a year. It runs about $20.00, but it may be of great help.

The Directory for Exceptional Children
Porter Sargent Publishers, Inc.
11 Beacon Street, Suite 1400
Boston, Massachusetts 02108
(617)-523-1670
Includes about 3000 schools, facilities and organizations across the United States. Both public and private facilities are covered – boarding schools, outpatient clinics, and residential and day facilities.

BOOKS

A Difference in the Family: Living With a Disabled Child
by Helen Featherstone
Viking Press 1985
A wonderfully frank discussion of family life with a member who is disabled. Helen's own son had toxoplasmosis. Can be heavy reading at times.

After the Tears:
Parents Talk about Raising a Child with a Disability
by Robin Simons
Children's Museum of Denver, 1987

Bringing Out the Best in Your Baby
by Art Ulene, M.D. and Steven Shelov, M.D.
Macmillan Publishing Co. 1986

Challenged Parenting
by Bonnie Wheeler
Regal Books 1971
A handbook for both parents and friends of the disabled; easy reading and uplifting.

Children With Cerebral Palsy: A Parent's Guide
edited by Elaine Geralis
Woodbine House 1991
One of the best all-around resources I have found to glean information. It is a very thorough guide discussing everything from emotions to advocacy, and includes a most comprehensive resource list.

Everyone Can Win
by Anne and George Allen
EPM Publications, Inc. 1988
Opportunities and programs in the arts for people with disabilities.

Handling the Young Cerebral Palsied Child at Home
by Nancie R. Finnie, FCSP
Plume 1974
This one has been around for a long time. A classic reference book for parents, though a little dry at times. Most helpful in explaining the proper way to physically handle the child, and in describing a wide variety of adaptive equipment, how to make it and where to buy.

In Time and With Love, Caring for the Special Needs Baby
by Marilyn Segal, Ph.D.
New Market Press 1988
One of the more practical, easy to read resources available, including sections on day-to-day child care, discipline, developing motor skills, and more.

Infant Massage
by Vimala Schneider McClure
Bantam Books 1989
Many of the massage techniques described in this book are very helpful for children with physical disabilities.

Negotiating the Special Education Maze:
A Guide for Parents and Teachers
by Winifred Anderson, Stephen Chitwood, and Deidre Hayden
Woodbine House 1990

Nobody's Perfect
Living and growing with Children Who Have Special Needs
By Nancy B. Miller, Ph D., M.S.W.
Paul H. Brookes Publishing Co. 1994
Discusses the emotional aspects and interpersonal relationships of parents of children with special needs.

Planning for the Future; Providing a Meaningful Life
for a Child with a Disability after Your Death
By Mark Russell, Attorney
American Publishing Company 1996
The author has done a good job keeping this reference current with new editions. It is a must-have resource if you are serious about protecting your child financially in the future.

Raising a Child Who has a Physical Disability
By Donna G. Albrecht
John Wiley & Sons 1995
This is a very practical guide based on real life experience. Topics include working with professionals, dealing with hospitalizations, and improving family relations.

Smart Toys for Babies from Birth to Two
by Kent Garland Burtt and Karen Kalkstein
Harper and Row 1981
77 easy-to-make toys to stimulate your baby's mind.

Special Parent, Special Child
by Tom Sullivan
G.P. Putnam's Sons 1995
Parents of children with disabilities share their trials, triumphs, and hard-won wisdom. This is what support groups should be all about – parents who have been through the trenches helping other parents. Great book!

Your Child Has a Disability
A Complete Sourcebook of Daily and Medical Care
by Dr. Mark L. Batshaw
Little, Brown, and Co. 1991

Your Child's Self-Esteem
by Dorothy Corkille Briggs
Dolphin Books 1975
This is a must-have book for any parent, but especially for those of us whose children need an extra dose of love and acceptance.

OTHER RESOURCES

Family Village
Waisman Center
University of Wisconsin-Madison
1500 highland Avenue
Madison, WI 53705-2280
www.familyvillage.wisc.edu
This organization has great links to numerous national, state, and local resources as well as communication opportunities for families.

Family Voices
 PO Box 769
Algodones, NM 87001
(888) 835 5669
www.familyvoices.org
A good information source concerning children with special health care needs.

National Council on Disability
1331 F Street NW, Suite 1050
Washington, DC 20004-1107
(202) 272 2004
www.ncd.gov
Here you can find out the latest on legislation for persons with disabilities, as well as get copies of such important governmental actions as the Americans with Disabilities Act 1990

National Parent to Parent Support and Information System
PO Box 907
Blue Ridge, GA 30513
(800) 651-1151
www.nppsis.org
If you want to connect with other parents or with parent to parent service organizations in your area, this is the place to turn. They can tell you whom you can contact.

Special Needs Project
3463 State Street, Suite 282
Santa Barbara, CA 93105
(800) 333-6867
www.ncd.gov
This is the parent's answer to amazon.com. They have literally thousands of book titles that will help people with special needs and their families.

Dana & Her Family

photo by Michael Libutti

About The Author

Author Janet Morel was suddenly and forever transformed when she became the mother of a young daughter with severe and multiple disabilities, including cerebral palsy, microcephalus, hydrocephalus, and blindness. Despite the tremendous challenges facing her family, she has developed a remarkably victorious and upbeat approach to life with her daughter. She is known for her freshness and candidness as a guest speaker for numerous workshops and seminars on Disability Awareness and on "Maintaining One's Sanity" as a parent of a child with disabilities. Ms. Morel appeared on national television on the Dr. Dean Edell Show, and is parent adviser for The Toxoplasmosis Research Institute. She currently lives in Kansas with her husband and two daughters and continues to be an active advocate for persons with disabilities and for their families. She also executed the mechanical drawings that appear throughout the text. This is her first book.

About The Illustrator

Francois Poisson obtained his BFA from the Rhode Island School of Design and his MFA from the University of Michigan. He works as a teacher and studio artist in Rhode Island, where he lives with his wife and two children.

INDEX

C

cassette player 28
cerebral palsy 34
Chitwood, Stephen 130
cognitive skills 29
computers 33
County fairs 39
Covey, Stephen 8

D

dance 36
Directory for Exceptional Children 128
Disabilities Rights Education/Defense 91
Dote-Kwan, Jamie iv, vi, 53
drawing 36
drinking
   with straw 34

E

equestrian riding 38
estate planning 95
evaluations, keep records of 70
Exceptional Parent Magazine 128

F

faith, importance of 13
Family Village 132
Family Voices 132
feel-y quilt 25, 46
feel-y quilt, directions for 47
Ferris wheels 39
fine arts 36
Fine Motor skills, developing 30
Finnie, Nancie R., FCSP 130
fish 21
Flaghouse 35
floats built into swim suits 35
food

R

reading 63
rhyming sounds 63
rhythmic dance 36
Rifton 37
roller coasters 35
rub with textures 22
Russell, Mark 131

S

safety pins 32
Sammons Preston 128
scooter board 39, 58–59
sculpting 36
Sculpting Dough, recipe for 48
Segal, Marilyn, Ph.D. 130
services 69
Seven Habits of Highly Effective People 9
Sharpening the Saw 9
Shelov, Steven , M.D. 129
sight 19
sign language 63
Simons, Robin 129
Sjostrom, Cheryl iv, vi, 43, 49, 54
skills
    cognitive 29
    fine motor 30
    verbal 64
sled 39
sleep 15
smell 26, 63
soldering, tips 52
sound 27
sound as vibrations 30
sounds 64
Special Needs Project 133
Special Populations by Flaghouse, Inc. 128
Special Populations Catalog 35
straw 34

Notes